Coming of Age on a Porn Set:

Trafficked In Hardcore Porn at 14

"Sometimes in the fight,
we find the warrior we always were."

By

Jewell Baraka

Copyright © 2024 by - Jewell Baraka - All Rights Reserved.

It is not legal to reproduce, duplicate, or transmit any part of this document in either electronic means or printed format. Recording of this publication is strictly prohibited.

Dedication

I dedicate this book to every person with kind eyes and extended hands who helped me heal and find my voice to speak my story.

Acknowledgement

I want to acknowledge and thank Exodus Cry for helping me find my way through my trafficking trauma by providing counseling, tools, a safe space to begin writing my book, and, most of all, for their friendship.

I want to acknowledge the book *"The Basics of Story Design"* for helping me to clarify and work out the writing of my story.

Finally, I want to acknowledge all my coffee shop homes along the way where my writing developed.

About the Author

Jewell Baraka is a writer, survivor, advocate, MMA enthusiast, beach lover, and seeker who has fought through the caverns of her own trauma to find a way forward both for herself and others.

She now uses her voice alongside other survivors and advocates to shine a light on the needs of survivors and the human rights violations in the sex industry.

For the last three years, she has worked as a crisis response Survivor Advocate, connecting trafficking victims identified in Los Angeles hospitals with resources, referrals and care to empower them on their way to a new life.

Table of Contents

A Note About The Music Referenced In My Book: 1
A Note About The Poetry In My Book: 3
1. Backstory…Snapshots To Lead Us In 4
2. Another Night At The Studio Begins 11
3. I Am Your Father - At Least In Title 17
4. Spinning A Magical World With Her Eyes Closed 24
5. Trafficked At 11: A Black Hole Forms 30
6. Entering The Matrix Of Porn 43
7. My Premiere...A Moment Of Shattering Light 46
8. Surges & Shorts 54
9. Another Night Of Shooting 57
10. The False World Coming Over My Eyes 62
11. Nowhere To Run For Help 68
12. Crumbling 71
13. The Mystical Warrior Poet And The Church 73
14. The Church Shoot 78
15. The Night Bleeding Into My Day Life 82
16. The Cage Fight Begins 87
17. Rising To Fight 93
18. A Trick Of Filming 97
19. Collisions 100
20. Into The Shadow 105
21. The Final Face-Off 111
22. Who Will Define Who I Will Be? 115
23. The Final Scene 122

24. My First Freedom Moment	127
25. Final Escape	130
26. On The Beach	134
Epilogue: Writing To Speak	142

A NOTE ABOUT THE MUSIC REFERENCED IN MY BOOK:

Music became a form of emotional expression long before I found my voice to speak my story. I was captivated by music from the start, even before I started sneaking it past my conservative parents.

My mom played classical piano, and she often would say that I jumped inside her when she practiced Chopin. I later learned to play Chopin myself, and the emotional release of playing his dynamic grand escalations was exciting, but classical piano was her dream, not mine.

Up until my pre-teen years, my music was mostly not of my choosing. But a whole world of music opened up to me just as my trafficking began. In it, I found a world of emotion that I didn't have to define. I could just agree with it and let it speak for me. And agreeing with a song brought much needed release for me and even connection in otherwise alone spaces.

I rarely like songs that don't speak to me, but this speaking is not just in words. The music is every bit as important as the words in evoking an emotional response. And my life always has always had a soundtrack that reflects more than just the popular bands of any era.

I like most musical styles outside of country and rap, which are just not my thing. But the soundtrack for this book moves mostly between rock, industrial, alternative, metal, and indie, with a random blues song by my fave, Nina Simone, thrown in.

My music has always been an emotional journal of sorts, so it was important to include it here. But don't get lost trying to nail down a timeline or chronology of the songs. The songs I reference in my book are often attached to some piece of my story during the healing that came much later.

You cannot heal or process while you are still in danger because surviving often requires numbness and a focus on immediate action, which makes it harder to be raw. So much of my processing of these moments happened years later when I was physically safe and far away from the land of my trauma.

That is why the soundtrack is not representative of the timeline of my story, nor are they in chronological order. Healing is not a straight line. It is more of a wormhole that takes you in and out of the corridors and caverns of your past trauma as you are ready to face different dimensions of each memory.

Because of copyright laws, I only reference the titles of the songs and describe how I connected to each song as I reference throughout the book. I created a Spotify playlist for my book. The Spotify Playlist title is: **Coming of Age on a Porn Set Playlist**, and it is under my profile: **Jewell Baraka**. The songs on the playlist are in the order that I mention them in the book.

For the Kindle version you can also click the link here:

https://open.spotify.com/playlist/3ZCQy7n0GRTsTHxGEFQ0Ht?si=wCh5c-JkRTuheTSZPlf3yg&pi=u-yNAl5OLRTiuA

A NOTE ABOUT THE POETRY IN MY BOOK:

In a gray, numb world that cared little about what existed beyond my mirror, camera or external character, I found writing in the form of poetry when I was 15. No one had told me it was ok for me to have feelings or to be human, so I had very little emotional vocabulary. I understood the meaning of the words that represent emotions, like anger or grief or pain, but not in relation to the movements happening within me.

Poetry, and writing in images became my way to make sense of the world inside me and ultimately created my own unique emotional vocabulary. The poetry was raw emotion being expressed. There are snippets of my poetry included throughout the book to connect you to the most raw, emotive expressions of me. All the poetry used in this book is my own.

I do reference once without quoting "Do Not Go Gentle Into That Dark Night" by Dylan Thomas.

As a survivor and an advocate, I believe in the power of a single story. I believe that when we put all the individual stories of sex trafficking and human rights violations in porn together, we will finally see a mosaic that reveals the full picture. All the names and some identifying details have been changed. The point of telling my story here is not legal prosecution. The statutes of limitations have long since passed. The point is the power of a single story. This is my story…

1. BACKSTORY...SNAPSHOTS TO LEAD US IN

The light of a film projector shining on the big theater screen woke me up one night when I was 14. As my eyes adjusted to the flickering light, I saw myself up on the screen, center stage, in a hardcore porn film. I had been sleepwalking through the last three years of my life, which is not to say that the last three years had been easy. Sometimes survival requires a numbing denial of the hard realities we are caught in, especially when we are engaged in command performances where our participation is required.

This robotic existence may have been partially induced by a lack of sleep but more from a lack of control. My dad was a controlling psychopath who spun his image masterfully, charming the community around us and even his church. It was his world, not mine. I don't know if it is a man's world or not anymore, but I know I was trapped in a man's world then.

And I also lived in the world of sex buyers and porn producers, which is another man's world. Yes, there are madams and female porn producers, but they are a token few held up to justify this man's world as balanced and egalitarian when it is anything but that.

My father dropped me into this world. I was caught in his narcissistic, psychopathic world first.

My father trafficked me when I was 11 into a brothel. I don't know the backstory of that. He was clearly a psychopath or sociopath, though he never went to a therapist for me to confirm my amateur diagnosis. In my nonprofessional assessment, I have landed on psychopath rather than sociopath because of his meticulous, calculating, cold, and yet charming way of navigating life.

Perhaps this glaring brokenness of person and character is the only real answer I need to answer the question of why he did what he did.

Some children are sold by their parents to a trafficker who takes them away from their home, and that act requires cruelty. My father did that night after night. He would take me from my bed and put me in the back of their car.

There was money exchanged. I saw it when the agreement was made, but there was also a void inside him, a coldness that allowed him to do this night after night without blinking or swerving.

My everyday life had the appearance of freedom. I went to school every day, got decent grades, and played sports and classical piano. But none of that made me actually free. There are many types of existential prisons and many ways to duct tape our mouths. You can't see all of them, but they imprison us in our trauma and silence us nonetheless.

I was raised into exploitation. I had been navigating my way through prisons all my life.

And I felt them around me nearly every moment. In the beginning, I lived in two main prisons: the prison of my mother's imaginary perfect world and the prison of my father's oppressive control over me.

When he trafficked me at 11, it wasn't the act that shocked me. I had seen the true man behind the mask at age 7. And it was not the act of sexual trauma. I had been sexualized since I was 5. His sexual education had taught me that violent rape was what I, as a girl, should expect from men.

So, though the sheer volume of men who wanted to rape a young girl every night shocked me, the repeated sexual trauma seemed normal. And through the twisted education of my father, I actually thought I might be fulfilling my purpose and place as a girl in this world.

My father's sexual abuse began when I was 5, but his BDSM-type torture with a serial killer-esque edge did not start until I was 7. Wanting to rape me but frustrated that my hole was too small that day, he hung me by my hands in the closet and stuck a knife inside me.

It was not a logical act for a normal mind, but to him, it made total sense. When I started to bleed onto the carpet, he flew into a rage. Mad that I was bleeding on the carpet, he rushed out of the room and returned with cleaning products for the carpet.

Instantly, I saw the man behind the mask and realized he could kill me without regret or conscience. His need to maintain his good guy persona was the only thing that stayed on his hand that day and in the days to come.

That was the moment I became a fighter in the "Hunger Games" world that was my life then. I resolved that day to oppose his direction for me, a direction that would surely end in my death.

Sun Tzu says, "To know your enemy you must become your enemy." I did not have the absence of heart and conscience to become a psychopath, but I was raised by one, so I learned his ways. He always conquered me physically and won in that way, but I would scream in his face defiantly, and I would never cry or show any weakness until he left the room. So I won too.

To reveal weakness to a psychopath is dangerous. My well-acted bravado and his need to maintain his pastor persona were the survival threads keeping me alive.

But the trafficking changed all that because it changed who my enemy was. It multiplied my enemies exponentially and I had to learn to adapt, to change form to survive.

At the brothel-type warehouse that I was trafficked into at 11, my bravado and defiance did not protect me; it endangered me. One night they put a gun to my head for defying a customer, for refusing the asshole some perverse sex act.

At that moment, I knew that my enemy had changed. Success survival would require something new of me at the brothel. This enemy was not my father, and I needed to learn who this enemy was to prevail.

Nothing was personal at the brothel. It was all business. Making a lot of money was the goal, and they did it well. There were at least 20 underage girls like me a night on the weekends who were purchased by an average of 8 men each night. You do the math.

This enemy wanted transactions to run smoothly, customers to be satisfied. If I kept customers satisfied, I would survive. The way to keep them happy was to understand what drove each man then I could satisfy them and thus survive the brothel.

I didn't need to be emotionally present inside to sense their broken drives and align myself with them. It was a process to learn how to see what they needed, but once I got that down, I could just see and shift into auto mode.

My sexual education with my father meant I didn't play innocent well, so the guys they sent to me mostly fit into two categories. For one type of sex buyer, I was the wild girl, the nympho, and for the other type, I was the bad girl who needed to be punished.

Both of these roles prepared me for my next command performance in hardcore porn.

Once I had these roles down, my life at the brothel went into auto mode, and the sleepwalking through my exploitation began.

Because the brothel had a focus on young girls when I was 14, in their view, I was beginning to look too old, so they began shopping for a new place to traffic me. Unfortunately for me, my sexual education thus far made me a perfect fit to be trafficked into hardcore porn.

And that is how I woke up one night when I was 14, trafficked into the hardcore porn industry.

To begin my porn story, you need these few snippets, snapshots of my life to make sense of it all, but I will tell these stories more fully as we go forward together.

One thought as we begin my porn story:

"The only purpose for which power can be rightfully exercised over any member of a civilized community, against his will, is to prevent harm to others. His own good, either physical or moral, is not sufficient warrant." **John Stuart Mill**

Possessing the power and the lack of conscience to inflict harm does not justify the harm. And this power to act without censure does not ever revoke our human rights. We are human beings, and we have a right to live free of harm. I have and had a right to live free of harm, but sometimes, we forget that until a shattering light breaks into our reality and wakes us up again.

But we are not quite to that moment in my story yet…

Armor covering
Hidden depths.
No exit, No entry
No light of day allowed in
Until now.

My pen
An armor-piercing knife
Extracting raw reaction
Writing with infrared eyes
My story shrouded in darkness
Until now.

My story
An incendiary armor-removing device
Unearthing buried depths
Revealing with words of light and fire
The story that neither you nor I
Wanted to hear
Until now.

Jewell Baraka

2. ANOTHER NIGHT AT THE STUDIO BEGINS

Through the overhead light glaring in my eyes, I can see a backlit man come through the haze into view as I emerge from the trunk of the car. The driver's job is done, so this man working the door will take me from the car through the studio door. Blinking back the light, I slip into numbness for another night at the porn studio.

<u>Cue music:</u> Send the Pain Below by Chevelle, a moody, alternative rock-feeling song that alternates between a pain-filled voice and yelling, reflects my internal voice as I slip into deep numbness. Now, all you can see on my face is blank bravado and steel.

The massive gray building emerges out of the dark space in front of me. I think it used to be a dry dock for repairing big ships before they converted it into a porn studio. It is a massive porn universe divided up into different sets that are always shifting.

I follow the doorman, clenching the old blanket that smells like car oil tightly around me. It is the only bit of clothing covering me, and I will only have it for a minute more. There is no escaping the night that lies before me. I don't hold any of the controls in my life. So I just go where the day or night takes me and navigate the danger the best I can.

Two massive heavy doors part and slide open as I approach.

<u>Cue music:</u> Minefield by Prodigy blaring its aggressive, industrial, slightly ominous rhythms play as I walk into the looming, vast, but chaotic space.

This night blends into the blur of almost every other night at the porn studio. Trauma spikes are the only thing that makes one night stick out from another.

At the door, Greta, a beautiful, efficient, 40-something woman with blonde hair, green eyes, and a slight German accent, is waiting for me. I doubt Greta is her real name. Everyone goes by stage names here. I am guessing that was hers when she was in the industry.

Porn is always looking for the new thing, the new spin on a sex act, the new girl. She is not that anymore. I wonder sometimes who she was at the start, when she was where I am now. She is my handler or assistant, depending on how you look at it. She is the person who moves me through each night on the porn set, from entrance to exit. In this world, she is part of my normal.

She takes the blanket off my back, hands it to the doorman and simply says, "Later," as she waves him off with the back of her hand. At the brothel, I was used to being essentially naked, with a g-string and heels, but I am still not used to walking through the crowds of people on set in this state.

I feel old beyond my years. My survival is entirely on my shoulders, and the weight of the fight against the harsh world I live in has aged me aggressively. I have never really felt like a teenager despite my 14-year-old physical age, but perhaps an awkward 14-year-old does remain somewhere within me, beneath my heavily armored exterior.

A stream of people in various states of nudity walk around the studio as everyone prepares for the night. Most of them look blank, blase, almost bored, though there is always an escalating anxiety of expectation as the start of the shoot comes near.

At first, they threw me into crowd scenes, orgies. It wasn't like a frat party, a rave or a love-in. It was sexual trauma from the front and the back by 10 different people in the first take. And somehow, I felt lost in the oblivion of naked bodies, completely invisible, while I was being sexually violated so violently.

At the brothel, I was in a room with a door. When the door opened, I knew I just had to survive that man until the door opened again, and he left. My time at the brothel was all about the moments between the door opening and closing. There is no door like that here.

The porn studio does not really have boundaries or dividing lines to break up the sexual trauma other than takes, but you never know how many takes there are to go. We shoot one night at a time, but that is a pretty long boundary when you have a barrage of men violating you from every side over and over again.

Looking around, mesmerized by the chaotic, sexual circus, I pause too long. Greta places her hand forcefully on my back and starts pushing me forward. "Ready, Candy? " she says in a questioning tone, though we are already in motion.

Candy is my stage name. It sounds sweet, but the glint in men's eyes when they say it makes me a little unsure of that initial interpretation. No one uses my real name here. Honestly, I don't think they know much of anything about me, but then I don't know much of anything about them either. Dialogue and sharing your story is not what porn sets or porn films excel at.

Time here always runs on fast forward. Every night in the porn studio is like a high-speed train without brakes. As soon as I walk through the door, I am hurled headlong towards whatever is coming at me that night.

Hair and make-up are a momentary reprieve before it all begins. The room is harshly lit, intentionally bright so they can see and disguise your every imperfection. People circle around me to apply makeup to my body and face. I spread my arms and legs wide so they can fix all my parts as I fade to gray. Going gray screen, numb, is the most common response in my life.

Still, being in the center is better than my early oblivion in the crowd orgy scenes. I remember the night the director called me over, a few months in, and said he wanted to make me a star.

In the middle of all that, he saw me or said he saw me, and that is what hooked me. I was not a performer by nature. I didn't have any inherent need to be in the center of things, but like any human person, I did want to be seen.

No one really sees you in the sex industry. They are in you and on you, but they don't see you, not really.

On set, they like that I am young, but they wish I had the rack of someone much older. So they shape and tape me up until I look like I do. When they are done, it feels tight and odd. And with the teased-up hair and heavy makeup, including my usually cherry red lips against my ivory skin, I don't really recognize myself in the mirror.

I am lost in the mirror void for just a moment, but I snap back as I see Greta out of the corner of my eye. Time to move a couple of rooms down to costumes, which is mostly a room full of racks of costumes and shelves of shoes. Costuming is a quick stop, like a revolving door.

Red lips and red shoes are a recurring theme for Candy, my character. Tonight's shoes are red Mary Jane's paired with white above-the-knee stockings. I usually just pay attention to my shoes because they are what I will have on the longest.

Am I becoming Candy? Is that what I agreed to that day with the director? It was all a little vague. Mostly I responded to being seen and was hoping for a new way to survive in this hardcore porn world.

The scene each night can be literally anything. I can never imagine what is coming. I never watched any kind of porn, let alone hardcore porn, before I was trafficked into it.

Tonight, I am essentially playing my nympho role from the brothel but dressed up like a schoolgirl. And that is all I really know as the shoot begins. If there is a line or two of dialogue, they will tell me when we get there. Mostly, they want me to smile and laugh no matter what happens until the final scene.

The vibe of this shoot is sexually playful, with an edge of incest. I have a ponytail and styling that makes me look a few years below my 14 years.

Having lived through three years at an underage brothel where most of my buyers were my father's age and now shooting this scene, I have to wonder, "What is the deal with old men wanting young girls? Why do they want girls their daughter's age? Why don't they want their wives and girlfriends? Do they do this to their own daughters the way my father does to me?"

Usually, they try to make me look older to pass as an adult, but that is not what they want tonight. And they always get what they want.

The strange thing about porn is that while I and other women are on the receiving end of their camera lens, it is not really about us at all. Men write the scripts here. Porn is the working out on film of men's erratic relationship with sex, power, and themselves. We are just pawns in their angst-driven existential processing.

Don't let the schoolgirl costume fool you. This kind of shoot, like every other night here at the studio, is not fun, playful or remotely sexually fulfilling for me. I start each night with a pasted-on smile full of energy, but every night, I end in a crumpled heap on the cold concrete floor, shaking and shivering.

<u>Cue music:</u> Shivering by Illenium, a slightly gothic, electronic, sounding anthem full of pain radiates its icy reflections as I will myself to move, to stand.

Suffocating
Under dark, murky waters
Flailing,
Reaching to rise.
- *Jewell Baraka*

Greta always helps me stand and walk off-set each night as my legs buckle in exhaustion. She is also responsible for giving me a sponge bath before I go. Not sure if this is nice or some version of erasing the evidence. But either way, it feels soothing, and it signals that the night is over and I have survived.

After that, the blanket I arrived in reappears with the doorman, who walks me back to the car.

3. I AM YOUR FATHER - AT LEAST IN TITLE

At the end of each night the same two men that drove me to the studio drive me home.

Home means lots of different things to different people. That word is sometimes associated with warmth and safety, but mine is not one of those. Home is just a different, hostile world to navigate.

When the trunk pops open, I see my father's steely, icy blue eyes staring down at me.

<u>Cue music:</u> Silhouettes by Smile Empty Soul, a post-grunge ballad with a jagged-edged, metal tinge, plays as my eyes meet the vacuous, cold emptiness of my father's.

Inky black midnight stands before me
There is no limit to the pain he adjudicates
Does his reign in my waking nightmare have an end?
- Jewell Baraka

He is the master of this universe, although his strength is in his calculated scheming and cold brutality, not in his stature or brute strength. He is 5'6 sleight of stature, but strong with wiry black hair. He is most powerful in the persona he wields and the people he moves like chess pieces around his board. He sees life as a game, a win/lose scenario, and he is always positioning himself to win.

He projects a charismatic yet humble, even caring, persona into the world that most people see him through, but I only see a vacuous emptiness covered in metal. He can cry on command, but it is more of a performance than an emotional response.

Actually, I have only ever seen him cry from the pulpit when he was preaching. It is fair to say I learned my distrust of preachers from my father.

He uses the pulpit like a weapon to secure his position and destabilize ours. As soon as I am old enough I start helping with the children's ministry just to get out of his sermons. He is always telling stories of our weaknesses in just the right light that makes him look benevolent and makes us look like broken fools. He spins himself as the hero while he weaves the webs of a villain around us, imprisoning us in his world.

The church is definitely his world. Whether we live in his world or the fantastical world of my mother's delusions is always muddled in my mind.

He is a pastor, a community leader, and a Kiwanis, and he is on the family counseling board, which is ironic since he doesn't believe in therapy. If you met him, you would infer his quiet manner as humility, but you would be wrong. His image is his central drive, and to mar or challenge it in any way is the quickest way to trigger his rage.

He feigns emotion and uses the rules of religion as a constructed conscience to project into the world, but he does not seem to feel actual guilt or emotion.

Nature or nurture? I do not know how he became the man that I knew. He certainly was not connected enough within himself or with his past to speak the history that would have helped me put his pieces together.

In poetic terms, I have always described him as metal, and when I tried to move from the poetic to the substantive, I described him as sociopathic for many years. Now, I would say that his methodical calculating nature is a sign that he was most likely a psychopath, though that is only my amateur opinion as I am not trained to make that kind of diagnosis.

When I use the term psychopath, you probably see pictures of some serial killer movie or TV show, of a man in a darkened apartment alone, surrounded by pictures of his victims. And I did watch serial killer movies and shows at one point in my healing to understand the mind of my father. But he never looked like the people I saw on those shows. He looked like the guy next door, the pastor of your church, part of the boys club in your community.

His persona was convincing. I believed his persona, too, for the first 5 years of my life. For a couple years after that I wasn't sure if I was seeing clearly. But once the mask came off, I could never see him that way again.

The only humanity I remember glimpsing after that was when he would watch old slapstick or Western comedy shows. His laughing would get so intense it became inaudible. He was completely immersed in the moment. And in those moments, I glimpsed for a second the boy inside, who evidently wasn't strong enough to overcome the metal man.

It was a very small piece of him by the time I met him. I don't remember ever feeling connected to my father. There are pictures of us before age 5 that appear like there is a connection, but I don't remember feeling connected to him. And our whole life was staged, so the pictures could have just been part of that performance of our family.

I don't think there was enough humanity present for me to connect to even before the trauma began. Once it began, I constructed a fortress between us and never reached for him again.

It was not safe to reach for him again.

I first got a glimpse behind his mask when I was 5. He started playing games with me where I ended up naked, and then he would quote strange bible verses about "whores" that I didn't understand. It felt like a dark storm came into my life at that time, and everything seemed unclear for the next two years.

I sensed, despite my desire to be good, that I clearly was not. Maybe it had to do with me being a girl. Even that young, I seemed to pick up that in this world I was born into, girls were to blame for men's sexual misbehavior, even their sexual crimes.

I was never sure why I was bad when I wanted to be good, but the feeling of badness was distinct and feeling as a child is what your reality is constructed of.

We progressed through stripping, staring, touching, berating, and finger insertion to him partially inserting himself into me in the next couple of years. The mask was slipping, but I was lost in the turbulent storm and unsure what I was seeing.

And then, one day, when I was 7, the mask incinerated, and the psychopath behind the mask finally emerged into the light of the day before me.

That day, in the middle of our usual "sexual game," he grabbed me, dragged me across the floor, and hung me by my wrists from the closet bar. He momentarily closed the folding wooden closet doors, leaving me hanging there naked. When the doors reopened, he was holding a knife.

I was not inside his mind that day, but looking back, I think he was frustrated he could not get his penis inside my 7-year-old body. In his broken logic, he decided that the solution was to make the hole inside me bigger. This was a solution not connected to empathy or the reality of the harm it would cause me. He stuck the knife inside me as if he was a surgeon. He was not.

As blood began to run down onto the carpet, he went ballistic. I had never seen him that angry before. He slammed the closet doors and stormed out of the room. When the doors re-opened, he was holding cleaning supplies to clean the carpet, which he did while I hung there bleeding.

That was the moment that I knew he could kill me without remorse, and that changed everything. I had been crumbling, emotional, and overwhelmed by this new dark storm for the last two years. In this instant, though, I saw what I was up against, and I knew that I couldn't crumble and survive.

So, I stopped crumbling. I became a warrior in this post-apocalyptic "Hunger Games" type world that I called home. After that, I never backed down from him. No matter what pain he inflicted in his BDSM-type closet sexual torture games, I fought wildly with bravado. Despite my fear, my eyes flashed an unwillingness to be broken by him.

The pain no longer crumbled me; it ignited my will to fight.

After that, when he hurt me, I would rage at him and would never crumble until he left the room and I was alone. He taught me many lessons about life in the negative sense. In this moment, he taught me to never show weakness before psychopaths and sociopaths.

His nature in my eyes never changed from that moment on. It only evolved and changed forms. At 11, he trafficked me and sold me to men who would sell me in their brothel. I saw money change hands for me that first night. It was an initial payment, I suppose.

I continued to live at home, but whenever they wanted me, my father would put me in a car with two men who took me to the brothel. That was the deal. So he was my trafficker in the sense he received money for me performing sexual services, but he never went to the brothel or, later, to the porn studio with me.

We often see stories overseas of men selling their daughters into trafficking. In those stories, they often go to live in the brothel away from their family of origin. In those stories we see the tragedy of a girl being sold by her family. And selling your daughter or relative is a sociopathic or psychopathic act, even if the family is impoverished.

But I think it takes another kind of man to put your daughter in the car with traffickers night after night for six years. What kind of will does that take to look in my eyes night after night and send me off into sexual violence? It reveals that there is a will that could have been used to heal himself but instead was used to solidify his brokenness and psychopathology.

Where did a man in his position find these men? I don't have the answer to that. We didn't exactly have long, in-depth dialogues about his life and mine. Someone clearly stepped into his life that connected him to this other world and network of commercial sex.

I have always felt that besides the money, there might have been blackmail involved. Perhaps they had something on him. He was a pastor, and I know he used porn as a teen. Perhaps that habit came back, and someone found out about it. Perhaps someone found out that he was abusing me.

Those are my best possible projections of a pieced-together backstory on my trafficking, but the truth is I don't know how I ended up in their car every night other than that he put me there.

Away from the pulpit, he was never a very verbal man, and he was a very broken man. As far as I saw, he never healed, so he never had the emotional connectedness to put together his life, which means there are pieces of mine that I will never fully make sense of.

I learned to work on the puzzle of me with the pieces I had and not to worry so much about the pieces I did not have. What I do know is that he never wavered in his resolve to continue sending me into the vacuous black hole of sexual violence as he trafficked me in prostitution and porn night after night.

His persona was the charming, humble, pastor and community leader. Behind his mask, the man I knew from age 7 on was made of metal, a psychopath that I was only connected to in fear that I hid from him well behind my own mask of bravado.

In my healing process years later, I was often asked, "Have you forgiven your father?" My repeated response: this question erroneously assumes that forgiveness is a one-time event. For me, forgiveness is a lifelong practice of accumulated moments of seeing the truth of the harm inflicted fully and deeply, as well as the fallout from that harm in my life, releasing the ashes of all of that into the winds, and then rising up, turning my back on what was, and walking away.

4. SPINNING A MAGICAL WORLD WITH HER EYES CLOSED

So, where was my mom in all this? Well, she was spinning a magical world for us to all live in, most of all herself. Imagination was like her superpower. She had a child's heart but the skills of an adult to weave an imaginary world around her and, for a time, around us.

Life had radically disappointed her. After all, at 19, she had married a pastor, which in the world she came from was like winning the lottery. She grew up on a farm in the Pacific Northwest, and in small-town life, pastors were like the center of the community.

That may be why she missed the signs. I wasn't there, so I don't know what they were, but there are always signs. I do know he was 11 years older than her, meticulous, very OCD, and hypercontrolling, so there are a few signs she might have missed. She was probably spinning her fairytale meets Little House on the Prairie world for herself even then.

She presented as a very capable woman. She could organize any event you gave her; she taught grade school Sunday School, led music at the church, and always planned some big adventure for our summer. She was loud in personality, and she always acted publicly like she was in charge, not under anyone's control. But inside, she was a child. I am not sure what her emotional age was, but I am guessing 7 or 8.

Christmas was the height of her delusion. From the day after Thanksgiving through Epiphany, we lived in a world full of lights, garland, cookies, elves, and all the delusionally happy pop Christmas Tunes like "We Need A Little Christmas" on endless repeat. As a kid, it was enchanting and hopeful. I couldn't help but be captivated by her and her child's view of the world.

Maybe she needed the hope, too. Maybe that is why she focused so hard on this one annual season. She was driven every year by a need to perfect it. There was little downtime until every bit of that year's Christmas plan had been fulfilled, usually after Christmas dinner.

For a while, I believed in her Christmas, though it was all a little too busy in activity, too garish in decoration, and too hyper-happy on steroids for me. I was a reflective, deep kid who preferred the beauty of the choral candlelight Christmas Eve service, watching the fire crackle or staring up at the winter sky absolutely covered in stars. But I went along with it all until I was 9 because that was when I finally saw the truth of this world she was spinning.

When I was 9, she walked into my bedroom right in the middle of one of my dad's sadistic sexual games with me. "Finally, someone will save me. Finally, someone will be on my side," I thought as I saw her walk in.

She just paused and looked back and forth between the two of us for what seemed like an eternity, but it was probably only a couple of minutes. I waited for her to cry out or hit him or grab me and run out of the room. But after a couple of minutes, she simply backed up and closed the door behind her. In that second, my world and her world around me exploded into a million pieces. And I never saw through her eyes again.

I have replayed that scene in my memory a thousand times wanting it to end differently, but it always ends the same. So I resolved to see every piece of truth, no matter how hard, so that I would never become captive to a pretend world like she did.

She was never the same after that day either. Her fantasy world, which may have started as a child's fun, now became a solidified prison that held her captive. Through the years, I watched her world get smaller and smaller. When you have to exclude everything that doesn't reconcile with the world you want to live in, the walls of the room you live in keep shrinking.

<u>Cue music:</u> Hallelujah by Jeff Buckley plays its haunting heartbreak, projecting a day years later when I would break a Hallelujah Christmas ornament in half to reflect this ending with her. It took me years to recognize that she was gone and let her go, but in truth, she never returned from that day when I was 9. I count it as the day she died.

The towering firs
Sense the raggedness within me
Beckoning the wind to bring its sway
To ground me in its soothing maternal rhythms
As I scream STAY!
- Jewell Baraka

I knew that day when I was 9 that survival was all on me. No one was coming for me.

With her bound up in her delusion, there was no barrier at all between me and him, nothing to protect me from what was to come. With her out of the way, he could take me from my room every night without challenge.

Everything shifted and crumbled after that, including our relationship. Without the connection of living in her world, there was only music between us. She had wanted to be a classical pianist but had never realized that dream. So, when I loved music and playing the piano, she spun her dream around me. She said I used to jump in her womb when she played one of Chopin's Polonaises, and years later, I would play it myself.

She taught me classical piano until I was in high school, and for a long time, it was how I felt approval from her and a connection to her, especially after that day when I was 9. We shared a love of music, but the styles we liked diverged from each other the older I got.

She liked country and gospel, classic pop, of course Christmas music, but mostly she liked Christian music. When I was younger, this was fine. Like every young Christian girl then, I liked Amy Grant, but the older I got, the more trauma I went through, the less I could connect to the pop Christian lyrics.

These singers seemed to live easily resolved "shiny, happy people" lives, and my life was nothing like that. That was the life my mom projected, but that was not actually her life, and it certainly was not mine. If you watch documentaries about Christian music artists, you will probably see that it was not theirs either.

By junior high, I had a radio that I hid, which was the beginning of my immersion into all kinds of music. And headphones became a salvation of sorts for me because no one really knew what you were listening to. I appeased the world she was trying to weave around me by leaving a piece of Christian music cover out while I listened to my music. But it didn't really save our relationship. We were hanging by a thread by the time I was in junior high school.

Unable on some level to exist without my father, she had blamed me for what she walked in on that day when I was 9. Many women do that...blame their daughters for their husband's abuse or other women for their husband's infidelity. When a woman calls another woman a whore it is usually that she is unwilling to face the truth of a man in her life.

My mother was the one warmth in my home, so when it went cold between us,, it was a dark day. I imagine it was dark for her, too. She likely didn't really know the nightmare she had married until that day when I was 9. And probably she felt trapped by his image and power the same way I did. Maybe she had always been under his thumb, and I just didn't see it.

He certainly was a man to be feared. I knew that better than anybody, but knowing that didn't keep me from feeling abandoned by her. She was surviving the only way she knew how, but one of the consequences of her choice that day was me being left alone to survive a treacherous landscape filled with sexually violent, dangerous men.

The magical world was gone after she left, as was the love. I never believed in magic, Santa Claus or fairytales again after that day when I was 9.

I did, however, hope against hope that she would return. She was the reason I remained attached, though loosely, to my family of origin for years after I got away. I was waiting for her to come back from that day.

The day I confronted my father 15 years after I left was not for him; it was for her to give her a chance to change the ending of that day when I was 9. I never expected that he would suddenly grow conscience or emotion or regret. I did hope that she would grow strong enough to believe me, to confront the truth and him and maybe even to leave him.

There would be no erasing of our first ending, though, and when I was sure of that, I finally let her go, acknowledging the finality of the death between us that had happened so long ago.

All my life up until the last time I talked to her, she would say that we had the "perfect family," but that was not even close to our actual reality. It was the reality she wanted, so she made it inside her no matter what that cost her.

I am not blaming. I am merely explaining so that you understand how I ended up being trafficked in hardcore porn at 14 with no one I trusted to speak my story to.

5. TRAFFICKED AT 11: A BLACK HOLE FORMS

So before we return to the porn studio, there is one more key piece you need: the trafficking, how it began and how life at the brothel led to being trafficked into hardcore porn at 14.

My father first trafficked me when I was 11. That first night, he stripped me in front of two men and took a stack of money from them. Not sure why they felt the whole scene was necessary, but it felt like a shift of worlds. Maybe that's why they did it, so that I would feel the end of my old world. It would not be the last time I felt that.

I spent that night trying to figure out what it all meant, what was coming next. I wasn't even close. I didn't have the imagination or the experience to foresee that summer, let alone what would come after it.

I was surprised when they took me home later that night after they had their fill of staring, groping, and raping me. Evidently, the deal was that they owned me now, but I would still live at home. My father was the enforcer of this deal, which meant he gave me to them night after night.

The first part of that summer was all about breaking me in, making sure I knew that the word no was not an option for me anymore. Any form of "no" was always punished with violence, humiliation, and pain. And that summer, they also taught me "the sexual skills" I didn't know.

This is certainly not the usual experience if there is a usual experience, for girls or boys who are trafficked in prostitution.

Polaris Project, which runs the national human trafficking hotline, lists 25 unique contexts or types of trafficking, both sex and labor, on its website. Each different context of trafficking will have its own characteristics and ways of operating. There is always some form of breaking and some teaching of expected behaviors, but the system I went through was unique to this trafficking scenario.

This summer was kind of like being in boot camp for the sex industry. The men running it were more brute force than brains, though. I got the impression that these men did this for fun, probably money too, but mostly because they enjoyed raping and breaking young girls.

<u>Cue music:</u> Welcome to the Jungle by Guns and Roses, with its party meets chaos, metal vibe heralds this new context of sexual trauma from men for me.

We started with stripping. I wasn't very good at it. I was never much of a dancer, and my body awareness pretty much sucked. They didn't push this skill too hard. There are plenty of men who don't care how you get naked as long as you do.

Their training methods were unique, to say the least. One night, they took me into a big room where men were seated in chairs all around the room. There were 20-30 men. They sat me down, straddling and facing the first man. And then just told me to lap dance around the room.

The men would slap me hard across the face if I did something wrong. They told me I couldn't leave until I made it around the room. It was a long night. There was another night like that for blow jobs, too.

My entrance into the brothel and the sex industry came through one final night of training in the art of sexual violence.

That night they tied me to a tree and lined up to commence a night of raping amidst their drunken party. The sight of a line of adult men waiting to rape me is etched within me. I certainly was not innocent at this point in my life, but still, it felt like they were reveling in the destruction of my innocence. That night was a foreshadowing of a fight that was coming for me.

I was being propelled headlong without brakes into a throbbing, spinning, high-speed car crash of body and soul pummeling me against the tree that night. The forceful pattern would rise again even stronger around me 3 years later in the middle of the hardcore porn studio where I was trafficked.

With each rape, the intensity amplified, and I faded further into exhausted delirium. I was counting as each one raped me. It was a way to manage the random chaos and pain. Whether or not they all raped me, I don't know because I lost consciousness at number nine.

When I woke up sometime later, I was lying naked at the base of the tree, and my body was still reverberating from the rapes. They were partying around me as if nothing had happened.

<u>Cue music:</u> New Medicines by Dead Poetic, with its punk rhythms and emo sentiments, voices the rage-filled tragedy of this moment as my insides spewed out along with a faint glimmer of possible healing to come on a much later day.

I run through the blue forest shaking
Flooded by a thousand pictures rustling within
Crying out on the winds to be heard.
*- **Jewell Baraka***

That night, unable to reconcile this injustice, I turned on myself. It was a pattern I had learned at home. Anger was only allowed for those who were male, and those who were female were always to blame for every act of sexual violence committed by men. The church protecting their broken men on pedestals solidified this reversal of the sexual blame pattern within me.

The rage that could not be expressed outwardly in this moment fueled the formation of what I would later call my self-destruct mode, a mode that began that night. This was the moment I became trash in my own mind, which perhaps was the final lesson they wanted to teach me.

And with the final lesson, I was deemed ready to graduate into prostitution at the warehouse, which was essentially an underage brothel.

The brothel was in a warehouse, an industrial building, next to one of the sloughs of the Columbia River just outside of Portland, Oregon. The outer walls were made of metal. The rooms were made with smaller partitions that didn't go all the way to the ceiling, which meant that you heard everything. To hear the harm of others is sometimes harder than the harm we are experiencing ourselves, at least it was for me.

There were two hallways of rooms with doors. And there were armed guards who were each responsible for a block of rooms. The prostituted/trafficked girls at this warehouse, which was run by men of Asian descent, were mostly white and Asian girls about 11-15 years old.

Just so you are aware, this is not the usual racial demographic according to most sex trafficking statistics. However, the racial composition of this brothel was dictated by the men running it and the buyers they brought in. Supply and demand may be an economic theory, but it is also the force that the sex industry runs on.

They ran the warehouse like a successful business with a definite organized crime kind of feel. I don't know if they were or not; I am just saying that it was a sense I picked up.

The summer of breaking had felt random and chaotic, but everything at the brothel was organized and operated meticulously, like clockwork.

Each night, I was taken out of the trunk of the car and wrapped in a blanket. As I walked through the front door, the guard always took away the blanket. We always entered and exited the warehouse naked. That way, they could be sure we didn't leave with any money.

The guard over our block of rooms would escort us to our room for the night. The guards took all the money and also escorted the sex buyers in and out.

My guard, as I often referred to him, was named Joe. He was built like a linebacker, a mix of Asian and Caucasian, with a scar over his left eye. He had a resting stern face and unreadable eyes. Perhaps it was this blank persona reminiscent of my father that connected me to him in all the wrong ways immediately.

Until we heal our trauma, we connect ourselves to broken people like those who broke us over and over again. I learned that lesson as I healed over and over again.

Joe, like every other man in my porn and trafficking story, lacks a backstory. Personal details and backstories are not shared in these kinds of places during this kind of sexual violence. No one wants you to know their personal details here, and no one cares about your own.

My guess is Joe had a family or at least a daughter, but perhaps they were not close. He seemed conflicted about how he related to girls. On the one hand, we were the merchandise, and he was a businessman or at least a worker in a very lucrative business, and he treated us accordingly. He was a serious man, and he tried to perform his function well.

This meant that despite the fact that we all wore just a thong and heels and were always mostly naked around him, he never took freebies from us. He did regularly slap us on our bare butts; however, in that rough place and context, those "atta girl" moments felt almost affectionate. His actual intentions, I don't know. It could have been just his way of getting young girls to fall in line with what his bosses wanted, his way of doing business.

At the warehouse, they expected each girl to fit into this tightly regimented routine, but my body and mind were not cooperating at the start. The gang rape at the tree had been an overload of trauma, like an explosion that short-circuited the connection between my mind and body. It was such an extreme spike that, for a time, it even disrupted my survival instincts.

Adjusting to the new world of the brothel-type warehouse was really not going well at first. I remembered the training, but it was distant inside me as if it had moved into a place I could not quite reach it.

Unable to shift into the mode the owners and buyers wanted, my frustration and their frustration escalated. Until one night, I inadvertently let down my guard and expressed my actual disgust at a buyer's perverse demand. Enraged, he dragged me down the hallway and threw me in front of the bosses, ranting loudly about "your worthless f**n whore bitch."

One boss just nodded to another man who stepped up and pointed the gun at my head. As he pulled back on the trigger, the boss signaled again, and he fired into the outer wall. Knocking me over the head with the butt of the gun, with complete calm and crystal clear coldness, he said, "If you do that again you are dead."

Message received loud and clear: "Conform or die." If I wanted to live, I would have to learn to play and conquer their game. Being raised by a psychopath, I had been taught that everything is a win/lose scenario, so I shifted immediately to understand and ultimately beat this one.

The need to survive immediately lifted the fog in my body and sharpened the focus of my mind. This clearing was important, but it didn't instantly solve the problem. My training, or breaking however you want to look at it, taught me sex acts but not how to discern what one particular sex buyer wanted and please them.

I was not a willing participant with my father, and being fire and not earth that was walked on is what kept me alive in our win/lose scenario. But the fire that kept me alive with my father would get me killed here. They wanted me to be earth, walked on with a smile, breathing merchandise that somehow knew what each man wanted and became it. Participation, not defiance, was what survival would require of me here.

What happened next would haunt me through my healing. I chose to play their game to at least appear to become what they wanted. But in my mind, that choice, if it was one, was a betrayal of my will to fight and made me responsible for every harm that followed.

I was 12 by this point and not in control of anything in my life or in this brothel. And if I wanted to live, this was the only path, but I wasn't clear on any of that then.

Survival mode in this place was about to change forms. The fear was enough to kick my body and mind into action, but learning to conform to each man's desires was not natural at all.

Survival mode is fight, flight or freeze. I couldn't run or fight without getting killed. So surviving required learning to freeze my will and subvert under the will of the sex buyer, at least until they walked out that door.

Freezing is not always inaction; sometimes, it looks like compliance or even consent. Isn't that what all the research on Stockholm Syndrome teaches us? To survive, sometimes we pretend for a while that our captors' will is our own. We sleepwalk through our lives to be what they want to keep ourselves alive.

<u>Cue music:</u> Sleeping Awake by P.O.D., with its trancelike melody and repetitive rock rhythm, proclaims the haze of numbness and disassociation that I now find myself in. That inability to fight straight out like I had fought my father disconnects me from myself. I play the role the bosses want, each man wants, but at what cost? I am living a vicarious, suspended life.

> *I am a robot in auto mode*
> *Going through the motions*
> *Trying to hide from everyone*
> *Especially myself.*
> **- Jewell Baraka**

In this new survival mode, I would have to merge myself into my buyer's desires, but there was still the problem of how I would know what each man wanted. I needed help to figure them out. I knew my father, but how could I know each man?

The information and guidance began to come to me through Joe. He cared about me and stepped in to save my life, whispering to me tips on each man before they entered. That's how I saw it then and for many years to come. But now I see that he was probably instructed to get me in line, bring me along however you want to say it, by his bosses.

Each time he whispered the preferences of the man about to enter, I felt a stay of execution and devotion to him as a savior in my life. But it was likely not motivated by care but rather by business necessity. I always called Joe my guard as if he was a protective person in my life, but the truth is the guards were to keep us in and keep the money safe. They were not to protect us, and I have no doubt that Joe would have shot me if he was ordered to.

Joe was a captor or at least a man playing a part in an oppressive system of sexual violence.

In the warehouse, each guard had a block of rooms. And for the most part we always went to the same block of rooms run by the same guard. My room sometimes changed, but the block of rooms I was in did not. So Joe was always my guard.

In a world that is unsafe, you often pick someone to trust. For me, in the world of the warehouse, the brothel, it was Joe I chose to trust. What I experienced with him is called "trauma bonding." I know that now. Then I thought he was the one person that wanted me to keep breathing and I wanted to pay him back for his kindness by performing well.

So, I worked hard to become what he hinted that each man wanted. After a while, my own senses began to tell me as I looked at the man standing in the doorway. If he looked angry or hungry, I shifted into the nympho role and expected hard sex. If he looked repressed, I shifted into the bad girl role so he could feel good about punishing me.

The more sex I had, the more my body's need for sex escalated, but that was just my body. Sex never seemed to be for me, so I never cared much about it all. I disassociated sex with each man just to get through the moments until the door opened again for him to exit. Sex, for me, was a flatline, numb at best.

The faces of the strange, twisted men, as old or older than my father, that the guard brought through her door each night all merge together in my mind. They weren't anything to me. Only the ones that caused me extreme pain or fear remain etched in my memory.

None of them filled me with terror like my father did, but they were not kind, desirable young men. Most of them were at least my father's age. Many of them were religious, which I knew by the crosses and collars they wore. Many had wedding rings on their hands. And all were consumed with themselves and their own personal angsty projections above all.

For me, it was a command performance, and that force, not desire, is what prompted my performance every night. The part of any victim of sexual exploitation is to act like you enjoy being raped, beaten, and humiliated, and I did. Seeing or speaking your actual feelings can get you killed in those kinds of places. I had learned my lesson well.

Scene after scene, man after man, I played out either the "nymphomaniac" or the "bad girl" that each man wanted me to be. In reality, I was neither. Still, the words "bad girl" stung, like a word being tattooed across my forehead, perhaps because they had begun their assault so long before with my father. In the midst of my disconnection, this projection of sex buyers to see me as bad instead of themselves still cut deep. Maybe this was because I thought they were seeing me as I was. They were not.

<u>Cue music:</u> It's Been Awhile by Staind sounding its grunge metal flow into my world, reflecting my distance and disdain from the world around me.

> *A thick glass wall*
> *Separates me*
> *From the outside world*
> *I see people moving by me*
> *But they are out of reach.*
> *Beyond the length of my trust.*
> *Even my image in the mirror*
> *Recedes from my reach.*
> **- Jewell Baraka**

Every moment I should have raged at them, all my buyers, my abusers, shapeshifted into cuts across my own wrists. The cutting was an addiction that would come later, but it began inside me in this time of disconnection from myself as well as the justice and humane treatment I was owed as a human person.

In my time at the warehouse, I developed a niche of sex buyers. My father's psychopathic twist on sexual abuse had left me used to a mix of sex and pain. Consequently, I was most successful with that type of sex buyers, and they soon started filtering these sex buyers my way. This initiated my rise to their version of success at the brothel.

Periodically, we were lined up for new buyers. We had a lot of regulars and some men they just assigned to a girl they thought they would like, but for those buyers with the most money, choice was demanded. So they would line us up and write numbers on our foreheads. Everyone knew the numbers indicated our popularity. I had a really high number, which indicated fewer requests at first, but by the time I was 14, a few years later, I was #3.

It was quite a mind fuck to feel success in that kind of place in a broken performance of their skewed projections of me. But affirmation was a rarity in that world at that time, so I drank it up, and it fed my conformations to their projected roles.

Since young girls were the attraction of this particular brothel, no one stayed at the warehouse much past the age of 14 or 15. I knew a change was coming as I reached that age.

We were not allowed to talk with the other girls, but our eyes would often lock as we passed each other in the halls. We spoke through our eyes loudly. I can still hear the echoes of screams that I saw in their eyes as we passed in the hall. And there were many faces that stopped appearing, but I never knew what happened when they never appeared again until it happened to me.

Evidently, at 14, I was starting to look too old, so they started looking for a new placement for me. At the underground S&M-type club and on the streets, I got a taste of what could be and where the other girls had gone, at least the ones who survived. None of these try-it-out nights seemed to fit me, so they sent in an expert, the one who knew me best there.

Over the past few years, my guard had brought man after man to sexually violate me, but never once, besides smacking my butt, had he touched me himself. Then, one night, he walked in, closed the door behind him, and while unbuckling his belt, he simply said, "Show me what you got." After we were done, he said, in a tone ironically rich with admiration, "You are one twisted fuck. I know just the place for you."

And with that, my fate was sealed. He had been sent to determine what would come next for me, and hardcore porn was his choice. In my wounded mind, he had saved me every night for the last three years. I saw him as a protector, so I had to believe he was paving a way forward for me, a way to future success. So I heard that I was being graduated, promoted to porn.

6. ENTERING THE MATRIX OF PORN

I knew little about porn when I walked into the studio that first night. I thought it would be like Hollywood without clothes or like the brothel with cameras, but I was absolutely wrong on both counts. There was no pulling the punches or penises. All the sexual violence was 100% real.

The circumstances of my life had not allowed me an education on hardcore porn before I was thrown into the middle of it. I lived in a dichotomy of abusive sexual expression on one side and repressive religious regulation on the other, which honestly is not that uncommon. More on that another day. This dichotomy, though, had left me blind with all of the sexually violating experience and none of the knowledge to go with it.

I arrived that first night full of energy and expectation. I was going to succeed here like I had at the warehouse. I would succeed and make them all proud, especially my guard, who helped get me here. I would have to thank him one day when I had conquered this world, too.

But that moment of bravado where I stood proudly projecting my own success in this land was disrupted by a crowd of men, a storm of sexual violence coming at me. Orgy scenes may be fun for the viewer, but being in the middle of them was not at all fun for me. Men inserting themselves into me from the front and back simultaneously, consecutively, but in a random pattern that I could not predict flooded and overwhelmed me.

It sent me into that feeling of rushing headlong at high speed without brakes that I had felt for the first time when I was gang raped as my initiation into the brothel. Lost in the oblivion of these orgy crowd scenes, I desperately searched for a tool to help me survive.

Trying to find a way back to a center within me, I just kept thinking, "Where is the door that opens and closes?" The door at the brothel is what helped me keep sane in that world. I did not have to survive the night. I just had to survive until the door opened again.

But where was the door here? The producer yelling cut was my only reprieve, but I never knew how long that would last or how many takes he would demand. The night was the only true boundary here, and that could last for hours.

On top of being propelled headlong into this frenzy of sexual violation night after night was this overwhelming sense of blindness, of not knowing how to rise up to survive, to succeed in this world. Who was my enemy now? What are the rules of this engagement, this war?

And not only was I blind, but somehow, in this world of cameras and naked people, I was actually obscured, hidden in the oblivion of bodies. I was not succeeding. I was failing. I seemed to be on the verge of another "gun at my head" moment, though I did not know what form it would come in this time.

And then, one night, a few months into this, a miracle happened. John, the director, actually saw me in the middle of the crowd and motioned with his hand for me to come over.

Despite my assessment of failure, he said, "You did well there, you are starting to get it. I see a spark growing in you, and I would like to develop it. I can make you a star. Would you like that?"

An enthusiastic but guarded "yes" was my response. I saw a narrow, dimly lit hallway of possibility open up, but my past experience brought the guarded understanding that the lights could be shut off at any time.

Still, there was a jump of light, hope, inside of me. I would blame myself for that response for years to come and believe that it made me culpable and responsible for everything that followed after that moment.

I had no idea what I was agreeing to, but in my mind, it could not be worse than the oblivion of sexual violation that the first few months at the porn studio had been. And he had seen me, like the guard, which gave me hope of a new ending for my life at the porn studio.

That is when he assigned Greta to me and when I started getting more attention in makeup and costumes. It seemed nice to be attended to, even if the process of having people correct all your less desirable body parts and caking my face with intense, colorful makeup felt odd.

The process was awkward, but being seen was a nice change of pace.

We are a few months from that moment now, and being center stage seems mostly normal to me now. I haven't seen the film we shot yet, but John said in a strange, slightly ominous tone that he would show it to me soon.

7. MY PREMIERE...A MOMENT OF SHATTERING LIGHT

The night began like any night at the studio. My handler met me at the door and put her left hand on the small of my back as if there were a force within her hand compelling me to move forward with her. And in the next second, we were off, moving at lightning speed toward and through hair and makeup.

Standing in makeup, people circling around me, attending to all my imperfections, I hear her sharp voice ring out, "Candy, we do not want to be late. The director wants to talk to you before the night starts. Now, let's go."

I stiffened a bit and stuffed any bit of my real self that was hovering around as deep as I could bury it. The porn producers were the only men that scared me more than my father. And after three years of being trafficked in prostitution, I had known my share of twisted, cruel men.

It isn't necessarily that these producers of porn are more cruel than my father or the other men I have known. They just have more power in a world that removes all the usual limits of humanity. This porn world has formed around an anarchy-like state of unregulated sexual expression, which in theory sounds like freedom, but whose freedom?

Unhindered sexual power in the hands of cruel men often inadvertently morphs into human rights violations. And this is the type of hardcore porn world that I find myself in tonight and every night.

When I walk onto set each night, it feels like a chaotic, dark circus, which is actually a scene from one of my porn films, but it is also an atmosphere. The chaos on set is not random, though. The chaos is sexual mayhem by design. Every moment is designed to elicit specific reactions in girls like me who really cannot act. Not that they care. They actually prefer the look of my real trauma, terror and pain.

The human girls, women, boys, and men that I see destroyed every night in this process are not just collateral damage. They are the point of the game each night for those scripting it. They win their game when we end the night destroyed.

As we arrive my handler nods to me and exits to the side. I am in full hyper-vigilant mode, scanning John's demeanor to try to anticipate what is coming next. I don't let him see that, though. One of the many things I learned from my father is that you never show your fear.

"I want to show you something," he says, walking through a swinging door. He doesn't bother to tell me to follow him. He knows that I will. He knows that his baited hook has landed in me. I delay for just a second to still the trembling inside and open the door with a burst of bravado.

Beyond the door is what looked like a windowless store filled up with X-rated movies. He picks one up and hands it to me. I stumble, my legs slightly buckling as I see myself on the cover of a porn flick. Of course, that is what we are doing here, but all this time, maybe in an act of self-protection, I have not taken the filming to the end product in my mind.

We can only delude ourselves so long before we like they said in the Matrix so articulately, we "see the world that has been pulled over our eyes to blind us from the truth." That moment had begun for me. There was no more hiding the truth from myself.

A wave of nausea hits me and John, recognizing this and strikes quickly. "Tonight is a big night. It is the premiere of your first porn flick. You can now call yourself a porn star," he says in a mocking tone of faux admiration and snide sentiment. And with a brief laugh in that same tone, he turns and walks back through the door.

My world starts spinning as the real world around me begins to break in, but there is no time to stop and take it in.

> *Shame,*
> *Swirling black holes*
> *Fueled by dying stars.*
> **- Jewell Baraka**

I feel compelled to follow him back through the door we came through. As I do, I see him a ways ahead of me, holding another door open. It is a room in the studio that I have not been in before. It is a screening room.

As I walk towards him, I am processing at the speed of light, trying to sort through this fog of denial that is breaking open inside me. I need to see what this means about me.

But the walk does not take long enough for me to even find a shred of equilibrium inside. My balance is off, and my bravado is crumbling as I walk through that door into the screening room. The room is dingy, musty, and dimly lit, and it smells like smoke, cheap beer, and sex, aka masturbatory emissions.

I enter the theater to mock cheers, chortles, whistles, and a crowd of invitations for blow jobs, quickies, and BDSM games.

I am standing in the back when this theater goes black. In the blackness, the room goes silent for just a second.

Cue Sound: 35mm Film Projector whose whirring and clicking at this moment felt apocalyptic.

But as the film projector clicks on and begins projecting its fodder, a loud, raunchy energy amps up in the room. Through the glaring and flickering of the film projector, I see myself up on that screen amidst drunken jeers and jacking off.

Candy Cunt: The Girl Who Likes to Fuck. That is the title. They don't see me, Candy, as sweet or as a star. They only see me as a fuck and a fool.

<u>Cue music:</u> Tourniquet by Evanescence releasing the vision of my harsh, twisted, confusing circumstances through their goth-edged hard rock and haunting vocals.

Perceptual world
As a glass ball around me - EXPLODING.
Shattered shards of tinged, tinkling glass - FALLING
To the ground
In a rising chime
Of dissonant clattering - SETTLING
Amidst grayish debris clouds
Into the landscape of pain
Soot, sand, and glass - CRUNCHING
Grimily underfoot.
Gray shell of caked mud
My deluded self - FALLING AWAY.

- *Jewell Baraka*

Years of necessitated survival denial are breaking open in this shattering light moment. It is so overwhelming that, unable to continue standing, I fall to my knees and start throwing up in the back corner of the room.

I have been sexually violated and humiliated for as long as I can remember, but I have never actually seen myself being sexually violated and humiliated before, except in my mind. Seeing this all on the screen before me is an earthquake moment.

I am usually skilled at hiding my traumatic experiences until I am alone. I am a professional disconnector and burier of my pain and trauma. It is the only way I have made it this far. To endure repeated sexual violence while going to school and church, where I had to put on a happy face, it was essential. It has been the only way to survive.

But in this moment, I feel all my masks begin to shatter, and boxes within me where I have hidden pain begin to crack open. I am casting off the remnants of the surreal life of disconnection and connecting with the reality of the hardcore porn world I now find myself in.

And seeing it so clearly is making me physically sick.

This pattern of throwing up as I confronted my trauma would continue throughout my healing. Throwing up became a metaphoric and literal way to get it out of me, away from me, though always carefully monitored so as not to become an eating disorder.

The men in the room erupt in mocking jeers at the sight of me on the floor throwing up. And instantaneously, compulsive masturbation breaks out across the room. Evidently, my humiliation is the gasoline that fuels their sexual fires.

There on my knees, throwing up, in the back of this smokey room that smells like sex, my eyes finally open to reality after the reality that I have been denying.

I am finally seeing the "desert of the real" behind the spin of this porn world. As they project me to porn users in sexual acts of inhumanity, I also see myself or my character; I am not sure which one. And I am not sure if I like either one. After 9 years of sexual trauma mixed with scripted projections of persona, I am not really sure who I am.

Captive to the screen, between fits of vomiting, reality comes to me in piece after piece of shattering light. There is no erasing this or flushing it from the corridors of my mind. This sexual trauma has been recorded on film for all to see across time.

The men in the room laugh voraciously at their "star" throwing up in the back corner. They like to watch falling stars. Every bit of my pain and humiliation excites and incites them to escalating bouts of compulsive masturbation.

That impulse seems to be a sense of conquest. Their domination is revealed in my crumbling. And I think possibly it is not just a domination of me, but a symbolic domination of whatever woman in their life they feel powerless over.

As my world continues crumbling, between bouts of vomiting, a thought breaks in. "These men are like my father." They intend extreme harm at least, and I sense that there is nothing holding them in line like my father's need to maintain his good-guy image.

What is the way out? I am spinning through the possible pathways in my mind. There is no one coming for me. My father, the pastor, has charmed everyone, so I know no one would believe me. They did not believe the daughters of the town drunk about sexual abuse, so there is no way they would believe me about this. And my mother is still lost in her fantasyland.

For the first time in a long time, I see the long view of what is to come and I do not end well if I continue on this road. I can no longer go with the flow and expect to survive inside and out.

The reality of what they are making me into in porn suddenly becomes clear. Everything that has been in my peripheral vision suddenly shifts in my line of sight. It is one thing to not see the truth, but having seen it tonight there is no going back.

Light to the poet and mystic in me is truth and hope. There is more truth than hope in this moment. Hope is faint and blinking like a dying neon sign, but reaching for it is my only chance of survival.

In the shattering light, I see myself through the lens of their film and simultaneously through my own accusing eyes while I simultaneously wake up to the harsh world of hardcore porn that I am immersed in. I see the trajectory of my annihilation that I am being hurled headlong towards. And I decide I have to stop going with the flow and fight for the spark of light and fire within me!

Matrix Eyes of pornographic men
Upside down skewed view
Mistaken for a mirror
Shattered mirror shards
Warped - reflecting and projecting
Not even remotely real Matrix reels

Ignite Phoenix fire.
- **Jewell Baraka**

    I resolve tonight that I will "not go gentle into that" dark night. I will "rage, rage against the dying of the light," in the words of my favorite poem by Dylan Thomas. The dark night here being the way all these men, these porn users and producers see me and spin me in their films as well as the literal death that is possible down this path.

8. SURGES & SHORTS

Back in the trunk for the ride home that night, I pull the blanket tight around me. There are no mirrors in the trunk, which I am thankful for.

I hate mirrors because I never see myself in them. I like vampire movies, and according to vampire lore, a vampire never appears in the mirror. Maybe I am the undead, though I feel more like the actual dead most of the time. Numbness is what has gotten me through my life so far, but that is about to change. It has to for me to survive inside.

Writing establishes a sense of self more than anything else in my life because it is just for me. I never show it to anyone. Around other people, I get lost because their needs are always primary, so I adapt myself to what they demand or need. It is hard to find myself in a mirror because I see all these adapted versions of myself and it is hard to sort out who I really am among all these adaptations.

Seeing my first porn film is like a mirror out of a nightmare where I appear as the worst possible version of myself. The light in me is strobing with both power and danger. I move through bursts of seeing, surging pain, and shadows of shame, all threatening to short me out.

I navigate the dangers of my life through instinct, through a sense of danger, and through seeing in the moment. But seeing the big picture is a whole different story. Everything is safer in disconnected pieces. This moment both threatens and offers to bring it all together, and I am not sure if I will survive that.

No one else has volunteered to take the blame for my life, so I always have. Because of this, the moment of shattering light that brings hope of what I could be also brings despair at what I have become and hurls all that blame at me.

Once I am back in my bed I crash into sleep for the couple hours I have left before school. I dream, as I always do, of the events of the night, perhaps reaching for a different ending to the story of this night.

But I wake up the next morning with the same story, the one I have not yet figured out how to escape. I always wake up exhausted. In the delirium of my lack of sleep, my days often feel surreal, almost dreamlike. The trauma of my nights is so great that there is little in the day that would shake me out of my exhaustion.

Once awake, I grab my blanket and lay down in front of the fire in the living room. I can take 15 minutes more. I know my father won't bother me here on the ugly green shag carpet with everyone scurrying about in the middle of their morning frenzy. So, I milk every minute of these early morning power naps.

I stretch it as long as I can without missing the bus to school. I like the bus, ok, as long as nobody sits by me. I can usually find a place close to the back and get lost in my music. U2 War is a good one that I have on perpetual repeat these days. I think the bloody war in Northern Ireland is a fitting metaphor for my life.

Once I get to school, it is a whole other world to survive, but compared to my nights, it is not so bad. Not that I want to live in the arbitrary world of high school social culture forever, but it will do for now.

In the midst of the cutthroat social network of junior high I learned how to not stick out in the wrong way. I didn't have the money to buy all the trendy clothes, but I learned to always get a couple of "on-trend" items so I wouldn't stick out. And I avoid jumping into any of the social outcast groups that would put me in the line of fire, though I am kind to every person from any group when we encounter each other in the halls.

My friends are not popular, but they are athletes and scholars, which makes them socially acceptable. That is important only because the last thing I need is trauma in my days as well. My nights of trauma are more than enough.

Walking the halls is the most unsettling time at school. It always feels like an episode of high school "Mean Girls" could begin at any moment. I am not the one being ridiculed or hurt here, but I do not enjoy watching that happen to anyone.

School is kind of like a break for me. No family or traffickers anywhere to be found. And I am just smart enough to be able to sleepwalk through my classes and still come out with the parental unit-mandated A's and B's. Mostly, I pretend to take notes while I journal, write, and let my mind wander off.

Walking through the surges and shorts of the sexual trauma of hardcore porn has made this freshman year feel like I was an electrified zombie in a German Industrial music video. Emotionally, I try to push down the trauma of the nights, but now it is refusing to stay contained in its box any longer. In that moment of shattering light, I could feel even the deepest buried boxes rising closer to the surface. I am still trying to find my way forward from all that came clear inside the screening room that night. I feel the bursts of fire and fight sparking within me, and that is powerful, but it also feels ominous because it is coming into all the shatterable complexities of my internal and external worlds.

9. ANOTHER NIGHT OF SHOOTING

<u>Cue music:</u> Come Out Swinging by The Offspring punching out its pummeling punk tune that fits my awkward but powerful energy meets anxiety bravado of the moment.

As I walk into the studio for another night of shooting, I hold my head up defiantly, like I always do, but inside, everything is different, shifting. There is no plan. My go-with-the-flow plan has just been obliterated. So now there is just improvisation, throwing punches and then bobbing and weaving as the world of hardcore porn comes at me.

Everything looks the same at the studio. I mean, the sets are always changing, but it is the same semi-organized chaos as usual. It is only me that feels different.

I have been sleepwalking through the last few years, but I am awake now.

As I walk into hair and makeup, I wonder what this part is really about. When I started shooting the film, I thought hair and makeup were about covering up my imperfections and making me look good enough to be desired.

But what got the most reactions at the screening were the scenes where I looked the most destroyed. If the goal is the crumbled, makeup-smeared, destroyed shots of me, what is this for?

Maybe it is like the bully who most enjoys wrecking the sandcastle that you have spent hours building. Maybe somehow, building me up makes wrecking me more satisfying.

Robotically, I move on to costuming as, not surprisingly, they put me in my signature, red again. The type of material varied, but the color rarely did. They said it was because I was "Candy, as in Candy Cane, who is sweet," but now I don't believe that. It is too bright to be scarlet, but perhaps it is like a flag for a bull, making me their target.

Looking around the chaotic, loud, sex circus in gray concrete that smells strongly of bleach with lights strobing obnoxiously, I wonder, "How did I get here?" That question felt so loud inside me that it feels almost externally audible, but it isn't. Everyone is completely oblivious to what is happening inside me.

I am not sure I see anyone at the studio as an ally, but if I had any doubts the premiere highlighted boldly the path they have me on and its treachery. No one here is looking out for me, leading me towards better things for me. No, their colors have been revealed: they are opponents, like my father, and we are set against each other. Like an MMA fight, there will only be one winner.

If I have learned anything from my father, it is to know my opponent and their game. Maybe I had pushed that aside for a time, but it is back center stage, in the front of my processing. I have to know what their game is in order to figure out how to win this game. And I have to know them. What are their weaknesses and limits? I have to know my opponent to have a chance of beating them.

I look around like I am seeing the studio and everyone in it for the first time. These are men, like my father, driven by a desire to conquer and inflict cruelty. They are more dangerous, though, because, in this hardcore porn world, they have the power to command whatever cruelty they envision. So this is not my father's world, and I know instinctively they are not the same opponent as my father.

I have no idea what these men do during the day, but clearly, they are not bound by the good guy image of my father. That is one thing I can use against him, to keep him in check.

I am used to living an invisible life. No one really sees me in my daily life. I mean, I have friends, but mostly, I blend into every setting and live a fairly invisible life. I have learned quite successfully how to hide in nearly every setting until now.

The film exposed me to myself but also to the world. There is no hiding now.

Hiding in any way is definitely off the table as a survival strategy. The only way to escape from this, with any shred of humanity, is to fight with everything I have.

"Candy, we need Candy," I hear John bark in the distance, and immediately the chain of reactions begins. Everyone moves when action is called. His voice echoes through the big, dark, empty spaces beyond the graphic sets.

"Candy, Candy...the name knocks about my brain. I liked that stage name so much at the start. It was a nice change from "bad girl, whore, rebel," and every other cuss word I was used to being called.

But it was just a trick that hits me now with a stinging slap across the cheek. When the titles rolled and I read, "Candy Cunt the Girl Who Likes to Fuck," I knew that I was back to being a cuss word. That was what they really thought of me as: a cuss word, a body part, and a fuck.

Naming me Candy had nothing to do with me being sweet in demeanor, like they said. Maybe they wanted to eat me, but nothing else about that name was what they said. It was just a trick that I fell for. For a girl who lives invisibly, my weak spot is a strong desire to be seen, which makes the premiere all the more confusing.

I am being seen, but it is the worst version of me possible. Just when I want to hide most, hiding has become an impossibility in this world, in the porn world and in my internal world.

I am always naked, but have never been exposed in this way, until now. I feel more naked tonight than I have ever felt before. The truth feels shattering, though possibly with a glimmer of a way out if I can find a way forward.

I have always loved stars, not movie stars, so much as the millions of stars in the dark winter sky. I wonder if a little girl in me heard that when the director had told me that night six months ago that he wanted to make me a star. I have never been the girl that needs to be in the center of the room, in the center of the spotlight, but I do want to be seen like a star in the sky.

The question now is, could I become the kind of star that I want to be, the kind that shines out brightly against the darkened sky? Or even short of that, could I just become the best version of myself that is possible?

As I am escorted towards the film stage I hastily shut down all the processing. No room for thinking just now, but fiercely, I determine I will keep my eyes open tonight and every night to come. I do not have a plan, but I know I can improvise in a fight. I have good instincts, though improvising this fight may require all the vision and instinct I have within me.

I toss Candy aside. She is dead to me now. I will answer to her on set, but I will not become her. I do not know who I am yet, but I will not let them write the script for my life one minute more. I will become the only writer of my life script.

The game is about to change drastically, and nothing will ever be the same again.

10. THE FALSE WORLD COMING OVER MY EYES

If I had learned anything about fighting from my father, it was that men, like him, viewed life as a game. People were just pawns in their game that they moved around to their best advantage.

Maybe it is sex that makes men crazy, or maybe mentally health-challenged men, and sex is a hazardous combination. It is hard to tell which it is. All I know is that the men in charge in this little corner of the hardcore porn industry seem to have more than their share of mental health concerns going on.

I was not a psychopath, but I had been raised by one, and I had learned to think like him in order to survive him. And now, to survive hardcore porn, I employed the same tactics I had learned from him. I tried to figure out their game and not allow them the end they wanted in me and my life. There was always a winner and a loser, and my life, inside and out, depended on figuring out how to win this game.

What game was I in now? I wondered. The game last time was to pretend they were making me a star, portraying me benevolently when, in actuality, they were making fun of me. They had made me the butt of their joke. But I didn't know it until I saw it on the screen.

The producer was bouncing off the walls with excitement at what he called a guerilla-style filming of porn, whatever that meant. They were calling this one "Candy Cunt Fucked in Real Life." That sounded ominous, but I wasn't really sure what that would look like in a scene. They never faked the rape or violence or torture here, so there was nothing to make more real there. It sounded like the plan was to shoot unscripted scenes, but I wasn't sure I believed it would really be unscripted.

In any case there would be no anticipating what was to come this time. This would be a fight of adaptation and improvisation, bob and weave and counter.

I walk towards the center of the set even as my brain is shifting into hyper-vigilant red alert mode; my eyes are darting quickly from side to side to assess the room.

It seems a little emptier than usual, absent the full crowd of cameras, actors, and noise I walk into each night at the studio. Right then, the director nods to a couple of men nearby, and each one grabs one side of me and throws me in the back of one of those old Chevy vans. This one is black with smoky windows.

As they do, I hear my handler shout in her slightly rough Germanic voice, "Watch the makeup and costume, please. Do not mess her up on the way there." Where is there? I wonder as the van door slides closed.

Laying on the floor of the van, it feels like the trunk of the car they always transport me in. There is more space around me, but in me, it is reminiscent of the spinning black hole I often feel on the way to the studio.

As the van stops and the door opens my adrenaline spikes. Whatever is coming, I am now in the middle of it. We walk into some kind of industrial manufacturing facility.

<u>Cue music:</u> Bullet with Butterfly Wings by Smashing Pumpkins with its darkly poetic, slightly prophetic words, singing and screaming of the coming doom for me in an edgy, angry tone that heals my soul through release. Actually, it would take years to get

to that release, but when I did, art and music helped me express and release my anger and pain in healthy ways.

One person starts checking my face and body. I feel like my body is covered with invisible handprints. They always handle me from face to breasts to butt as if I am a package they are preparing.

The film crew rushes around, setting up lights. It is a sign to me that despite John's speech about porn in real life, this would be staged, at least in part.

The huge industrial elevator doors open before me. They signal to me to walk in. I feel like a miniature of myself inside that large space, but I wouldn't be alone in here for long.

The glaring camera lights all switch on at once, and I am blinded for a moment, but the light coming on lets me know that the game has begun. The light reminds me that despite John's grandiose proclamations, this is not real life.

Because all the sexual violence and trauma is actual, not simulated or faked, I would later begin to lose a grasp on whether the scenes were real life happening to me in the real world or not. I clung to this moment; the lights switched on in a blinding fashion as my sign each time that, despite my pain, the scenes were, in fact, staged.

I feel men move into the space around me, but they are blurry at first. When I can see clearly again, I see about 10 men in blue uniforms surrounding me. There is only a breath of a pause before they attack like a pack of wild dogs.

Looking back, I am sure that many of the male actors in porn were also caught in a cycle of exploitation and possibly trafficking. I did not see them in that light then, though. They were partnering with the men in power in porn, violating and abusing me violently scene after scene. It is fair to say that I saw all men of porn as perpetrators then.

One man pins me to the wall and rapes me, and then pushes me back to the center so the pack can feed on me again. Rape seems to be the food they enjoy, or perhaps that is just how the scene was written. They are coming at me from all directions. And in this style of filming porn, we don't ever really ever stop filming, so it seems endless, like a marathon that keeps getting longer.

During the whole shoot the elevator keeps going up and down and opening and closing. And for a second, each time the elevator door opens I remember the brothel and start to breathe a sigh of relief as if this scene has finally ended. But just then, the doors close, like my mom closed the door on me, and the sexual violence from all sides resumes again.

This goes on for what feels like hours, but I do not know how long it really is. What I do know is that the tone of the night feels angrier than other nights. It feels like there was an elevated rage radiating through the gang rape in the industrial elevator that we are shooting tonight. Did they know I had determined I would fight their script for me? I am not sure, but something feels different.

The jail cell
Encases me
Glimpses of light
Are the most I see
The pain seers through my body
Frantically, I scan for exits
But it is a futile reach
This dungeon is a fortress

From which there is no escape.
- Jewell Baraka

The second to last time the doors open, I collapse into a heap on the floor. That is like a green light that amps up the energy in the room. When the doors close this time, they stand me up and attack me more intensely than they had at the start.

The last time the doors open after a pause is to fully capture the mess that I am. Once they do, the camera light finally switches off. And knowing that there is nothing more I have to do, I deflate and allow the film crew to carry me back to the van.

If buildings remember, I think my screams are still echoing from that elevator throughout that concrete building today.

My nights at the porn studio often involved gang rape, but there were cuts and stops and starts. Somehow, the direction and the cuts made it feel different. It did not change the number of men in and out of me, the physical exhaustion and pain, or the trauma I experienced, but it made it feel easier to disconnect from everything afterward. Maybe because they were putting it in boxes, I could too.

But tonight had not been like that. There was no box, only continuous sexual violence in what seemed simultaneously staged and connected to the real world to me.

I was already living a sexually traumatic reality, but this shoot took that to another level. I experienced it at least partly, as if a group of random men saw me and their gut reaction to me was vicious gang rape. The cameraman and his direction indicated it was still a shoot, so I had that fact to help me create a little distance inside myself, but it was not enough.

Later, the director would ask me, almost rhetorically since he didn't take a breath afterward, how I liked the new film. He seemed to like to hear himself talk, so he went on to describe this new style of porn again, which I totally tuned out. "I hear you stirred up quite a response tonight…men do like to eat their Candy," he laughed. And with that, he walked out of the room, leaving me to sort out the night and the game I was now in.

Maybe it was my young age and my emotional development, but whatever it was a tear between my perceptual world and the actual world began that night. It began to feel like I was in danger of random gang rape and sexual violence wherever I went. The world I had grown up in already felt hostile, but something about that guerilla porn style of filming escalated off the charts inside me.

Normally groups of men at work do not spontaneously rape a girl for hours in an industrial elevator. But I didn't really know that then. I was coming of age on a hardcore porn set, so this was creating my norm. All the rape, gang rape, violence, and torture are 100% actual in a hardcore porn film, so the fact the camera is rolling does nothing to actually mute or erase the sexual trauma.

And gender roles to me were essentially that men rape and women are raped. So this style of filming porn fit right into my worldview at the time.

Because I was a minor, then it is clear under the law that I was #TraffickedInPorn and that it was all a crime. But how would being over 18 have eliminated the human rights violations I experienced in that elevator? The presence of sex should not void our human rights, even in the context of porn.

Freedom ends where the significant harm to another human being begins.

11. NOWHERE TO RUN FOR HELP

The next porn shoot, I am back in the black Chevy van, pushed in hurriedly because we are running late. My adrenaline spikes off the charts as I try to anticipate what is coming next, but I don't know why I keep trying to see ahead here. I never really can. I am blind by design here, and there is no real workaround except to react.

I ready myself for whatever is next as the van screeches to a halt suddenly. I feel myself pushed out onto the street with the cameraman in one movement, and as the van door opens, the screeches off, though likely to just up around the corner.

I am standing there in my signature red platform shoes and fire-engine-red lips, waiting.

I do not know this street, but there are so many streets in a city you cannot possibly know them all. I look around, wondering what to do, but just then, as if on cue, I see a police car. I walk towards it automatically, not really thinking what I would say, but expecting help of some kind.

Right then, the lights siren goes on, and they screech to a stop in front of me. The two male cops quickly jump out, grab me, push me down on the ground and cuff me. I am so disoriented that I don't read this as the clear setup of a porn scene that it is.

Looking back, it is clear that everything that follows is scripted porn actors, but it takes me time to catch onto this. I internalized it initially as maybe a setup, but not a set. And I think that was exactly the concept behind this filming style: to make it unclear whether it was a random or a staged porn scene.

Once I am cuffed, they begin verbally assaulting me, talking dirty to me and feeling me up and down, but not in the frisking sense. "So you are up for it, are you? Just putting it out there for everyone to see," one fake cop said, grabbing me. "Well, we are going to show what we do to girls like that," said the other fake cop as he shoved his baton up my butt.

After violating me from the back with his baton for a few minutes while his partner attacks me from the front, they throw me into the back of their car.

I am glad for the few minutes of reprieve before whatever is coming next. By now, I am up to speed, but still wondering if this might be a porn version of COPS, partly real, partly not, but which part is real and which is not. The camera guy is still with me, so that's a sign for not so real.

When we reach what seems to be a police station, one cop grabs me roughly by my upper arm and pulls me into the station. It looks like the police stations I have seen on TV, but that is my only real reference point for authenticity. It is full of people and noise, but everyone seems to turn and look at me as we walk in.

The noise resumes as they exit the main room into the booking room. The fingerprinting part seems like every cop show I have seen, but the mug shots are a little different.

As I step onto the dot to be photographed, one of the fake cops says, "Make sure you get a full body shot on every angle for this one. We want to make sure we remember exactly what this little cunt looked like."

"This is not real," I tell myself over and over again, but I am not a hundred percent sure of that. If you have ever seen the movie The Matrix, you will understand how real illusion can feel at times. And when you add in the factor of actual sexual trauma, it gets even fuzzier.

They move me into an empty interrogation room, and instantly, it becomes clear what part of the scene we are in. I had shot enough porn scenes by now to know what was coming next. And just as I expect, cop after cop comes into the room to violate, rape, and physically assault me.

After what feels like a few hours of sexual violence, they push me back out on the street in front of the police station and take off the cuffs. And in one of the worst porn lines ever, one of the cops says, "Remember us next time you feel up for it cunt." It's unclear from the tone of voice whether that is a threat or an invitation, but likely it is both.

And with that, they walk back up the stairs to the police station. And a few minutes later, as if on cue, the van pulls up in front of me, the door slides open and it is back to the studio. Amazing that the cameraman was there to capture it all on video, wasn't it?!

12. CRUMBLING

The stupor of the blur that follows that shoot feels especially intense. I am always in physical pain, but this was more than that. Walls were breaking down inside my psyche, and I was frantically trying to keep them from crumbling.

My day world had always been divided from my night world. The rules of these worlds were different, so I separated them to keep myself safe and, of course, to contain the pain.

This film series we were shooting had started to crumble the wall between day and night. I am not sure why, but I can feel it. Maybe it is the appearance of real life in the porn shoots that is unnerving me; maybe it is just accumulated, escalating trauma that can no longer be contained. In any case, I can feel it rising, building to release like a volcano within me.

<u>Cue music:</u> Falling Away From Me by Korn, pounding hard metal rhythms and breathy, pain-filled vocals project the expression I don't have for my trauma-induced PTSD and crumbling of self and soul. And I breathe release at last at being understood.

I feel a thousand bullets ripping into me
Instantaneously I take off running
But their bullet supply is limitless
And their guns are always loaded.
So even in the farthest corners of my world
The bullets keep ripping through my body.
In this war
There is no shelter,
No place to hide.
- Jewell Baraka

I am in desperate need of rest and care, but there is not much of that in my world. There are moments of it in my daily life when I am alone outside watching the trees blow in the wind or the formations of clouds move across the sky. But it is never long enough to recover from the endless streams of trauma coming at me.

And before I know it we are preparing to shoot the last scene in this series. For me, this one would be the hardest, the one that took me years to process because it invaded a spiritual space within me, which was already a confusing space in my life. I was raised in the church, and my spirituality is connected to Jesus, but the church with people in it has always been a hostile space to navigate. It is a world that was neither safe nor a world I called my own.

13. THE MYSTICAL WARRIOR POET AND THE CHURCH

I have been a mystical warrior-poet from the start. I always had that animistic sense of the spirit and light moving through nature and that sense of vision in relation to the spiritual world. It is possible that I have some Native American blood in me. It is always whispered about as a possibility but never confirmed by the older generation that would know. To them, it wasn't something to be proud of.

For me, it isn't so much animals, but rather trees and sky and rain and the sea that are alive and connected to me. If you have ever driven through New Mexico, you know that skies do speak and dance. For me, growing up unparented, the trees extended their arms in a swaying rhythm to soothe my pain. And the skies speak to me of other skies of other worlds ahead for me if I can only make it there.

I am strongly connected to the spirit in the world around me. My mystical core is a bonfire blazing against the dark night surrounding me, shape-shifting at times into a torch to lead me through.

The poet in me helps to express my unique story. And the warrior is the fuel, the fighter that makes everything, including this present moment of breathing and speaking my story, possible.

We never emerge into this world fully formed, but these pieces of my core essence have been there from the start. And the mystical warrior poet that I am would not be the same without my eyes. My eyes always see through the bullshit around me, which isn't to say that I know anything beyond a shadow of a doubt.

My doubt of everything, including my eyes and my perspective, is constant and, at times, absolute. But as Rene Descartes said, "The beginning of wisdom is found in doubting; by doubting we come to the question, and by seeking we may come upon the truth." That path through self-doubt leads me through trauma towards the truth, the light of day.

I sense the bigger contexts around me even before I understand or can explain what I am sensing. In Kindergarten, I remember having a discussion about the upcoming presidential election. I am sure I didn't have anything truly insightful to say, but I was interested in that bigger context around me. At Disneyland, this place of pretend and fun, I was captivated by Great Moments with Lincoln. I enjoyed the rides, but that conversation is what lingered within me.

I remember stopping abruptly when I heard Martin Luther King's voice coming out of the TV screen for the first time. He was long dead by the time I heard him, but it was as if I could feel him coming across the winds to speak to me of justice, movements, and hope. I am not African or African American, and I never experienced racism personally, but I have experienced injustice and gender oppression. And I felt the fire and power in his voice igniting my own, though the release of my voice into the world would have to wait. No one wants to hear my voice at the moment.

My lifelong vision quest, the pursuit of truth, began early. It was temporarily sidelined by my need to survive the trafficking, but since the screening, it has moved back to center stage within me. In church, I am surrounded by people who see the world in black and white as if things are easy to figure out, but I always see the world in shades of gray.

We all have a culture inside our own personal space when we are alone. My culture is characterized by this mystical connection, vision quest, poetic expression, and the fight to live to speak my story.

That is my natural internal culture, but surrounding me is a myriad of other cultures. One of the most familiar and yet also, at times, the strangest is the church my father leads.

Jesus, who is the center of the Christian Church, has never been the issue for me. Jesus has been a part of my authentic spiritual world from the start, though no picture or movie I ever saw depicted the person I know. I remember seeing some bible movie and afterward arguing with my mom about who the imposter in the film was. The Jesus I know is made up of mostly bright light with extremely kind eyes.

Supposedly, we know the same person or being, but that is where the similarity ends. There is an old hymn we sing called "My Father's World," and the church to me is that…my father's world, though not the father the hymn intends. That is the biggest point of contention between us. Because this is the world where my father wields his pedestal, preacher power. The church is his world, not mine.

This is not a complaint, just an explanation. I am not sure it is a world I want to belong to anyway. I remember when I got baptized, this older lady with white hair greeted me with a towel as I emerged and said, "You have been washed in the blood of the lamb." I know what she meant now, but then I thought it was the weirdest, grossest thing to say…ever.

Every culture has a language, so there is nothing unusual about the church having a language; it is just an especially odd language at times that doesn't seem to fit me.

I like the singing and the food at potlucks. The berry cobbler is the bomb, but other parts of the church culture are a little more difficult to navigate.

I love sneaking into the old white church when it is empty and looking up into the sunlight filtering through the stained glass. In those moments, I feel that mystical connection of light and spirit, but as soon as that room is full of people, it is gone. The people bring a danger that I have learned to navigate but not erase.

This is my father's world, so every face within the reach of his voice, under his control, is dangerous. And the church is a world run by men, and men, in my experience, are dangerous so that adds to the danger of the world of the church for me.

In evangelical conservative churches like my father's, shame and guilt are often flung about as if they are benevolence when, in fact, they are a method of control. The church culture is full of shame, often self-inflicted shame at the request of the shared culture.

I have come to despise the word testimony because invariably, it is always a person shaming themselves, who they have been and then pasting a happy Jesus ending on it. I do not need any more shame, and I do not relate to that black-and-white character development with a shiny, happy ending pasted on. It is a story formulation that does not fit my life.

My world is filled with all the complexity of shades of gray. After all, my father, who is the hero of their world, is the villain of mine.

Judgment is the most recognized historical weapon of the church and, ironically, what Jesus condemns the Pharisees for in the Bible. This sharpness comes at me every time I step out of the church's allotted boxes, which is regularly. The black-and-white of religious thought has never fit well around the rampant, repeated sexual trauma and its fallout that permeates my life.

But I learned early when the structures of life failed me to step in and raise myself. So, I follow my own sense of spirituality connected to Jesus but not so connected to the church. I create my own unique patterns of culture infused with music, poetry, existential musings, and friendship with people inside and outside the church walls.

However, it is hard to see myself clearly or define myself. I navigate by this sense of light within me. And in spaces like nature or an empty church, I connect deeply with my sense of light. I just try to keep it to myself. That keeps this internal space as safe as it can be for now.

14. THE CHURCH SHOOT

I am sure John or whoever wrote the script for tonight did not know any of this when they wrote it. Porn loves to play on themes of religious people being naughty.

Like the last scene in this series this scene begins as the van screeches to a halt and pushes me out with a cameraman. The city block is quiet, lit by street lights and the light of the camera following me. I am looking down the row of houses when I spot a well-illuminated church.

Forgetting the sheer red mesh and red thong lingerie with red stiletto heels that is my costume tonight, I am drawn up the stairs to its door.

As I walked up the stairs to the church, I remember sneaking into the old white church with the stained glass near my house because I loved to see the light filter through the colored glass. I loved standing there by the huge stained glass window with my eyes closed and the light shining down on my face.

I click the handle and find it is open. So I gently open the door and step into the candlelit and incense filled room with familiar crosses. As I step in, I feel that sense of sacred space that the empty church always had for me as a kid.

I am lost in the candlelit peace and warmth when the door slams loudly behind me. And I am jolted back to the reality of the moment, which is a screaming priest. What is he saying? I tune back in to focus on his words but then jump back as I catch a reflection of myself in the brass and remember what I am wearing.

A severe blush of shame rushes over me from head to toe, and I begin to back out of the room. The priest pursues me angrily, following me all the way down the stairs. And finally, I begin to hear his words, "abomination and desecration and you blah blah blah."

He just keeps repeating those words as he chases me back down the church stairs.

> *Once I met a bright light with kind eyes*
> *But days of shivering on the cold concrete*
> *are shattering my own eyes*
> *This shadow world may be my fated end - or a consequence*
> *And I, a falling star thrown down to Earth.*
> **- Jewell Baraka**

Stumbling, uncharacteristically tearing up, moving erratically, I lose one of my shoes, but just so you know, this is not a Cinderella moment.

At the bottom of the stairs, I fall to my knees sobbing, hoping this scene is over, but it has just begun. A crowd of men appears as if on cue, and the priest yells to them, "We must show this whore her place." So, two men grab me and tie me to the streetlight.

The priest keeps ranting this diatribe about "showing this whore her place" as the crowd gathers around me. Then the priest pulls a knife out of his pocket, walks over to cut my thong off, and just nods. The raping and sobbing ensue as they "show me my place."

> *How can this shadow of death be the place that I belong?*
> *I falter as the stained glass dramatically shatters*
> *And I dissolve into scarlet stones and letters.*

- Jewell Baraka

The sobbing has little to do with the church or the porn priest. Somehow, I was caught off guard, and this invaded my internal space. Maybe it references the shaming bible verses that my father began our abuse with. It feels like the accusation got inside this time, though I am not sure how, and I feel my light and fire waning, flickering within as if someone has doused it with water.

<u>Cue music:</u>
I explode into a million pieces
And screaming erupts out of me involuntarily
The crippling pain crumples me
Into a lifeless heap
Lying in the middle of the road.
No one even notices I am there
As everyone moves around me
Ignoring my cries.
- Jewell Baraka

Safe spaces have always been rare in my external world, but inside, I always have always had places to hide, but they are dwindling rapidly.

I came from there, my bedroom at age 5, through prostitution at the brothel and into the world of hardcore porn. And yet somehow, in each world, the conclusion is the same: I am one to blame while these men committing crimes and human rights violations against me are respected, patted on the back, and even the ones that people in the community and church bring fucking cookies to.

Note: The world has changed a little for the better since then. #MeToo and #ChurchToo have helped release some of the stories, but there are many more waiting to be spoken. But all this I learned between there and here.

15. THE NIGHT BLEEDING INTO MY DAY LIFE

The dissonance between my two lives is getting harder to navigate. I had a process whenever I experienced the trauma of stuffing it down, hiding it deep so I could keep projecting this pretend normal life.

I learned early how to disassociate the trauma by watching a music box with a butterfly that turned. By the time it stopped turning, I didn't feel anything at all.

Since my trafficking began, the butterfly has morphed into the audible repetitive rhythm of the tires as my dissociative tool on the ride home each night. It is a neat trick, but my feelings are growing unruly now, and I am less compliant with the process. They are starting to bleed into my life in the day.

As the storm brews within me, I am becoming more reclusive. I have a small circle of friends, but many are consumed by boyfriends at the moment anyway, so no one notices my withdrawal.

Boys, in the romantic sense are the last complication I need in my life. I get enough of those, well mostly men, at night, but all those born male fit in the same category to me… dangerous. Still, to fit in with my peer group, I always make sure I am vocal about a crush, usually on a popular boy who I know is unattainable and out of reach.

Around the start of my junior year in high school, I started spending more time alone. I eat lunch and then find an empty classroom or some stairs with my headphones soundtracking my life.

I am emotionally illiterate. Nothing in my life has taught me that emotions are allowed for me. And so they exist in one big disconnected jumble within me that I have no idea how to categorize or sort out. But two things have happened recently that are changing that.

Last summer, for my birthday, someone who did not know me very well gave me a blue sky and rainbow-covered journal. I hate pastels and dress mostly in black. There is no goth or alternative Cure following crowd in my high school, but if there was, that likely would fit me best. But, though I hated the look of the journal immediately, something about its blank pages drew me in, and I began to write.

For the first couple pages, I wrote from my projected life, the life perhaps I wish I was living where my biggest worry is the next high school dance. And then it hit me that no one was going to read this unless I let them. When I realized that, I was like, "fuck this, I am going to write what I want." Of course, I hide the journal well. Reality and truth are not appreciated in my home.

The other thing is that a boy a year older than me killed himself recently. I didn't know him at all, but somehow, in trying to understand how he felt, I have opened up some dark caverns in my own depths. Day and night are merging into one now. And the landscape within me is beginning to flood with murky, undefined and yet stormy emotions.

They drive me to write compulsively. Luckily, teachers assume I am taking notes, which means that every class has become free writing time for me.

But that doesn't mean I have made sense of much yet. I understand the definitions of words that represent emotions but not how they connect to what is happening inside me. So I use images to represent what I am feeling inside, mostly in poetry, dark realism-focused poetry that has little whimsy and zero romantic sensibilities about it. My poetry is real in the sense it represents my insides to the best of my ability, but it is also obscure, so it is safe for me should someone find it.

I mostly hate mirrors because I don't see myself in them. I see projections and shadows and fears, but I never really see myself clearly within them. Perhaps I am part of the living dead who can never find themselves reflected in a mirror. There is nothing harder to see through all the trauma and pain than the mirror's true reflection of me.

But I am beginning to see pieces, and even the broken pieces of my mirror feel important. It is just the beginning of seeing, and I can only see a piece at a time, but it is a forward movement. All transformation begins with seeing.

My mom chooses not to see, and I watch the space she lives in get smaller and smaller as she excludes piece after piece of reality. I am determined I will not do that.

I cannot explain why each poem is an accurate representation of me, but I can feel in my depths that they are. I always know when I am done with a poem when I have expressed what I set out to write. But that does not mean I have any kind of map of my internal or external world. I have a few pieces of the puzzle, but there are thousands of pieces I still need. Putting them together may one day be the story of my healing, but I am miles and miles from that kind of moment.

So, as I write, I often feel simultaneously excited that I understand this one piece and simultaneously overwhelmed at this complicated, dangerous maze I am fighting to find a way through and out the other side into the light of day.

In action TV shows, I like to watch the stories escalate and then resolve. My porn films escalate too, but they never resolve, at least not for me. Maybe the scenes of mocking and pain bring resolution to the men on set or the men who will later watch my film, but for me, there is no resolution.

The elevator scene felt like an escalating explosion that went from 0 to warp speed in a few seconds. To write it in a poem, I would describe that scene as me dismembered piece by piece and strewn across the elevator floor as the door opens and closes without any closure.

My connection to feelings comes in bursts and snippets, but my writing is the truest thing I have. It feels like the only tool I have in the fight to figure out if I am the character they have spun me as or if I may be someone else entirely.

In and out, I fade through the day with snippets of traumatic intruding. I jump to attention only when someone's abrupt movement inadvertently triggers my hypervigilant self-protection.

Mostly, I hide in plain sight every day. Maybe because the cameras are focused on me every night, I want less and less to be seen. But my hiding started long before I was trafficked into hardcore porn.

Being a part of my family is a command performance every day. My father rules the land around us, and his image is his most valued prize. So, under threat of harm, we all have a role to play.

I don't really like to pretend or project much of anything, so I have learned to blend in and mostly live within my internal world in a defensive stance.

Being a pastor's kid who is always being introduced to people, I can do the first 5 minutes of conversation with anyone, but I usually forget their name before the conversation is over. They don't want to know me. They want to know him. I am only being introduced to them as part of the performance, so there is nothing real about that moment that needs to be retained. So, as I walk away, I dissolve the performance projection and return to my own space, the only space that is safe in this world I exist in.

Or at least that is how it used to be. I feel my own spaces becoming more stormy and less contained, but while the atmosphere is shifting, there are still safe corners and spaces within me for now.

16. THE CAGE FIGHT BEGINS

In hardcore porn, rushing headlong into sexual mayhem at a rhythm of off-the-charts escalation culminating in a violent crash is normal. So, it can be hard to describe spikes of trauma because spikes are part of the normal nightly process here.

It is the first night of a new film, and there is a buzz in the air. A new shoot setup is always like that. I am still swirling in the internal chaos from our last set of shoots. So I am distracted, lost in a swirling internal black hole stained scarlet, as I move through the motions of prep for the night. But not distracted enough to shut down my internal alarm systems or my internal shutdown process as I walk toward the set for the night.

The theme of the set this night seems to be a nightmarish circus. There is a macabrely decorated, rectangular animal cage on wheels in the center that catches my eye first.

Every system, world or culture has its rules. Hardcore porn is an upside-down world where the meaning of my actions and speech are opposite. My "No" or "Stop" somehow translates in their ears to "Go Harder" or "Push Further." When I act in what I believe is brave defiance, my actions are translated in their eyes into an angry, rebellious woman who must be put down, subdued, and tamed by whatever means required.

<u>Cue music:</u> Feuer Frei by Rammstein, the German industrial, releases its aggressive, chaotic, raspy sound to set the scene rising in me and around me. It may be a hard sound, but it fits the scene, and like my poems, matching a song to a scene brings a sigh of relief that there is an appropriate expression for my pain and others who feel the same.

Pounding hammers pulsate pain
Through my brain
Screeching schisms scream pain
Through my ears
Empty world entombs
My soul in the depths
Tortured dreams torment my rest.
- Jewell Baraka

"Where do you want me," I ask without thinking. "In the cage, of course," the director says with a mocking laugh that has a cutting edge.

I stand motionless for a moment, staring on the outside as I see in fast forward a projection of what this night will bring. Sometimes, in the past, I have frozen in scary moments, to a degree that worked in the warehouse where I was prostituted. But this is not that world, and I know that survival strategy will not work tonight. And with only me against a set full of mostly adult men twice my size, there is clearly nowhere to run.

Fighting with every ounce of strength I have within me is the only way to survive this night. There will be no flight or freeze tonight, only fight.

There is only a moment to prepare myself for the fight before me tonight, to become steel as much as I can in a minute. There is no avoiding the violence coming for me. There is only forward, only through to the final bell now.

So I walk with all the bravado I have within me as if I don't give a shit, up the metal ramp through the open door of the cage. A man with a black hooded mask down to his neck with holes for only his eyes, mouth and nose follows me in.

Once he is in, he kicks the metal ramp away and locks the door. As he turns to face me I see the bullwhip, stick, and another tool I do not recognize on his belt. "So this is to be a test of torture," I think. "Ok, this is a landscape of abuse, I understand,' I declare inside and rise, trying to take on the form of the white tigress who will fight to the end.

Some people crumble in physical pain, but I am not one of those, not anymore. The day my father stuck a knife inside me when I was 7, the fighter inside rose up. The extreme pain that day, combined with the danger I saw in his eyes as he coldly cut me, awakened my fight.

I have been fighting the script porn is writing for me, about me, since I saw the night they showed me my first film. But there is a different level of fight that activates me when I am physically injured or tortured that they have not seen yet, but they are about to.

I stare unflinchingly into the eyes of this masked opponent as I wait for the fight to begin. The cameras and lights are in place, which I see in my peripheral vision since my eyes are still locked straight ahead on his…and then I hear "ACTION" reverberate through the set.

The first bell sounds, and instantly, we begin to move. I circle opposite him in the square cage as he cracks the whip with a macheesmo flourish. I am not impressed. The cracking of his whip becomes the rhythm of our movement around the cage. Through the scripted eyes of porn that night, I am the animal to be tamed. But I am not tame.

I feel the blood on my legs after one of his cracks, and I know the whip has found its mark. I am disconnected, but on some level, I still feel the pain, and it incites the rage of the tigress, the fighter within. Suddenly, the fight shifts into fast forward.

It becomes a blur of cracking whips and me moving not away from him but towards him, screaming, enraged by the pain. Like my father before him, he seems excited by this.

Eventually, the whip snaps between my legs and crumples me, just for a second, but it is long enough for him to pin me down with his knee. "CUT," I hear from the left of the cage. "But don't move," John adds.

I look up into the masked man's eyes as he waits perched upon me; I see that glimmer like I have seen in my father's eyes a million times before. For a psychopath or sociopath, it is more satisfying to conquer someone who is fighting. Everyone else is just too easy to defeat.

To this kind of man, rape is a "prize" that they earn by crushing the girl who is resisting them. This "prize" is meant to prove their dominance, power and manhood. But they will not get that prize from me tonight without a fight.

"ACTION," I hear this time from straight ahead, beyond my feet. And instantly, the masked man jams himself inside me as I flail and bite and scratch him. He will not get his prize unscathed.

When he is done, as he is zipping up, he moves his leg, pinning me, and I jump to my feet.

Out of the corner of my eye, I see a rolling motion from the director, indicating for him to keep going. So the circling begins again, but he has cast the whip aside. Now, he has a stick-shaped instrument made of metal in his hands that has a red light on it and is making a whirring sound.

I am not sure what is coming, but I am sure it is going to hurt, so I move opposite him, back and forth, round and round.

When it finally lands I get the literal shock of my life. The jolt that went through me is off the charts. With every shock he lands, I scream louder in his face and alternately circle and lunge at him. The rage of the pain fuels me and simultaneously focuses me.

Often, rage is seen as an emotion of oppressors but not of the oppressed. But rage can be positive when it is a response to cruelty, to the desecration of all that is sun and ocean and sky within us. That day, when I was 7 when the warrior emerged, I was not choosing to hurt with my rage but rather to save myself. I was choosing, in the words of Dylan Thomas, "to rage, rage against the dying of the light" in me, physically and emotionally.

The cameras begin circling the cage as I rage around the cage, at times even grabbing the bars and screaming outward as if to accuse all my oppressors on set that night.

John loves this development. The whole set is roaring in approval.

The pain is so intense that everything in my vision is disconnected, and snippets of perceptions are coming in and out at lightning speed. Somewhere in these incoming snippets between rage, pain, and screaming, I start trying to downshift, but rage is a powerful drive that is hard to stop once you engage it.

I am caught in the flow of a fight against pain, against the crowd of enforcers on set, against the opponent before me, and against the forces of malevolent mayhem that I felt thrust into the middle of.

So the rage continues amidst a blur of different instruments of pain in a mix of fast forward and slow motion as I disconnect deeper and deeper. I finish the scene as if I am watching someone else who is not me.

The adrenaline is hard to stop, so I am still fighting, flailing even after I hear "CUT" again and watch my opponent unlock the door and jump down to exit the cage.

The director nods, and two men replace the ramp and come to get me.

As they reach me, finally realizing it is over, I collapse into a heap. They pick me up and carry me to my handler. She washes me, wraps the blanket around me, and walks me to the car, waiting to take me home for the night.

In such a harsh environment, I always receive her actions as care, but I realize it is also her job. And maybe part of her job is erasing the evidence of all this in case I ever do find a voice to speak. I don't know. It may be random sexual mayhem that is not that intentional, but then again, it may all be scripted.

17. RISING TO FIGHT

There are times when we have the luxury of licking our wounds and hiding away in a safe cave. This is not one of those times. There is no time to feel sorry for myself or attend to my wounds. Now, there is only the fight. And I am starting to think this might be a fight to death, one way or another.

What you have to know about this fight is that it has been rigged from the start. I have been a 14-17-year-old girl against a whole crowd on the set of mostly adult men twice my size, many of whom are writing the script, which are the rules of this fight.

The night I saw my first film, I decided to fight, having no concrete picture of how that would play out. I did not want to follow their script or their development of my character, which, in actuality, was more of a character destruction of me. When I chose to become a better version of myself, I knew there would be a high cost. But still, I could never have foreseen this.

I walked into this fight like a child warrior, full of bravado and the will to charge but without real physical power and skill to back it up. I was strong inside and skilled at adapting to the trauma before me, but I was not a skilled fighter on this level. There was little chance of winning the fight physically, so I just had to charge in, knowing that it probably was not going to end well, but I had to keep fighting until I either collapsed or the night ended, whichever came first.

This charging bravado, which looked like an angry woman to them may have been what they wanted all along. But while this was a porn flick, so technically a film, I did not have a script for moving through this experience of being trafficked in porn. So, I fought, adapted, fell, reacted, broke, and exerted every ounce of strength to rise from the ground I was being thrown to.

Our shoots usually went in sets themed so they could be compiled into a longer film. So, I expect more pain tonight, but I am not sure what it will look like.

There isn't much to the set tonight. The circus cage was gone. It was mostly an empty space. They always tape up my chest to make me look bigger than I am, but other than that and my thigh-high red boots, there is not much to my costume tonight.

The director motions for me to move toward the center of the empty space. Once I am there, he motions again, and a camera moves close to me while, at the same time, three costumed male performers move toward me. I cannot see what they have in their hands, but it seems to be connected to a leather strip.

When they get close, the camera is shining right on my face, so I feel more than I see the two metal clamps with sharp edges they place on my breasts and the dildo-like object with jagged edges they insert inside me. Both are attached to long leather straps, the other end of which is held by a tall masked male performer built like a football player.

The pain and resulting rage happen in quick succession. And before I know it, the man on the other end of the leather cord yanks it, and with a flash of excruciating pain, I know just how bad he can hurt me.

With every time he yanks and I stumble forward, bleeding, the crowd in a semi-circle around him jeers and cheers. I flash back inside to that night when they made me watch my first porn film with a room full of men. They jeered and cheered at my pain then, too.

The message of this scene is unambiguous. Dominance is being asserted, even flaunted, and my pain is their proof of their domination.

The only thing I can do now to fight is keep standing back up each time despite the pain, which actually takes every bit of strength and will and fight I have within me. "Maybe if I can hold out long enough, it will soon be time to go home," I think desperately. But that is a blind hope flailing in the darkness of my searing pain.

<u>Cue music:</u> Hemorrhage by Fuel reflecting the pain that had begun in me through the hard rock, straight edge with a tinge of metal, raspy-voiced song. Expressing the pain that I do not have adequate words for.

> *Deep, dark waters of the abyss lie before me*
> *In it I see mortal wounds from "Nazgul blades"*
> *Breaches - Caverns of pain*
> *Where ravens perch.*
> *Tortured enslavements of body and soul*
> *Exhausted collapse…*
> *Breakdown*
> **- Jewell Baraka**

And then I feel a hard yank and the worst pain I have ever felt as their clamps are ripped off of me. I collapse amidst a puddle of blood as everything goes black.

When I wake up in the scene following this, it feels like it has been hours. And the ripping, the injury from the last scene, has been sewn up. But we are not done, not yet. I wake up in excruciating pain in a dog cage, and it is certain there will be more to survive tonight if it is still night. Nothing is clear.

18. A TRICK OF FILMING

Note: What follows is a trick of filming. In the last scene, I was the warrior in my eyes, in their eyes, the angry woman, but in either case, I fought until I collapsed. Now they start filming as if in between that scene and this scene, they had broken me. No such thing happened, but for a long time into my healing, they fooled even me.

Waking up, I am disoriented, throbbing in pain, trying to remember where I am and what is happening. And I am without my bravado, which is usually my armor. The pain is deafening and blinding within me as I weakly open my eyes. Where am I? I usually don't usually sleep on the set or anywhere except at home. I feel so lost and fuzzy.

Then I started looking around. I am in a dog cage, just bigger than me, and I am naked except for a collar attached to a leash. Questions come spinning through my consciousness, heightened by the blinding pain. "Is the night still going? Is this my new life? Did I die? Is this hell," I wonder out loud.

My reassimilation processing is cut short by the entrance of a man. He is no different than all the other male porn performers, but the intense physical pain has stripped me of all my usual defenses, so he seems more menacing somehow. He feels like a caricature of darkness out of a superhero movie walking towards me.

I try to shrink back, but there is nowhere to hide. He opens the cage, grabs the leather strap and yanks me forward. I bang against the cage, just barely bigger than me, painfully as I fall forward onto my hands and knees.

"That's it, walk like a dog, you bitch," he yells, as the pain crumples me to the floor. He yanks me forward and then knocks me backward, where I land on my feet crouched down. "Beg, you bitch, beg," he commands.

I am still disoriented, throbbing in pain, and I really just wanted to be wrapped in a blanket and tucked into bed to sleep for a couple of days. Not connecting with his world, I just stare blankly at him. Angrily he begins to bark commands and take me through "bitch training drills," as he calls them, and the cameras circle around me, recording my pain.

The scene shifts as he pushes me down to "heel" to sit at his feet. He pulls the leash tight and turns to face me, opens his fly, and pees on me all in one motion.

When he is done with that, he has me get up on a table on my hands and knees to display my defeat, I assume. Then he shoves what looks like a billy club up my butt and violates me that way for a while because "dogs like it up the butt," he explains with a sharp laugh.

It is a long night. If it is just one, it feels like a couple of days at least, but usually, we only shoot one night at a time. Maybe it is the pain that is making it feel so long. I don't really know.

However long it has been finally to the end of that shoot, and I realize that this was just a long night or nights. It has not become my life or existential hell, however, you want to look at it. Eventually, I do arrive back in my bed, and I fall asleep, determined that my life will not end as Candy, the twisted porn character they are writing for me. I will survive to write my own character.

Note: As a warrior, I saw that night as a loss, as a called fight. What I didn't understand then is that a warrior is not defined by a single bout. A warrior has many fights across their life. Losing one fight does not define us.

19. COLLISIONS

I wake up in a funk of strobing pain, blurred vision, and a head full of fog and cotton. I call it my "harsh world" feeling.

The only way to survive this kind of trauma is to create patterns of habitual disconnection. You can't live in that excruciating pain, so you learn to disconnect from it, to bury it deep within you. I am living with a graveyard of traumatic moments inside while projecting the performance by day that I am part of the "perfect family,' my mom's words, not mine.

But sometimes the trauma is not compliant and lingers despite my attempts to bury it or even pops up without invitation. The "harsh world feeling" is a moment of this lingering or popping up. It is a deep connection to the pain from my trauma, a reminder of the graveyard that exists within me.

I have been immersed in the graveyard all day. I am grateful and relieved to wake up in my own bed and not on the nightmarish set of the night before. Still, I am stuck in the harsh world of last night, and I cannot shake the feeling that maybe this was not an end to the nightmare but a pause.

Whatever happens next, though, I feel grateful to have a pause.

All of our stories have fortunate and unfortunate elements existing together. Some elements in our life are both. My day life is often a performance, and there is pressure in that, but the time at school and time living in my shell of a life is also a break from the violent, sexual trauma.

This week, my day life is giving me my annual solo vacation: camp. I am not really an outdoor girl, but I discovered in 4th grade that my parents would pay for a week of camp once a year, and I was hooked. Mostly, I go for the week away, but the swimming, campfires, and canteen, aka candy store, are pretty cool too.

Arriving at camp I can't get rid of them fast enough. They linger and do the performance of hugs and tears for mom, but I just wave them off. "Write to us," my mom says through the car window. You can be sure I won't; I think inside and wave "bye-bye."

I settle in and begin to enjoy my break and see what kind of cabin mates I have this year. It is always a slightly odd bunch, but not dangerous, just quirky. Although one year, one of my cabin mates did steal all our canteen money, that was a bummer, but the camp gave us credits, so it all worked out. And I hide my money better now.

I always get to camp early enough to snag a corner-top bunk where I can hide away from the world. My survival skills definitely help me here, too. Besides my top bunk hiding space, there is the hot water issue. Only the first few showers in the morning get hot water. Once I realized this, despite hating mornings, I started getting up at 6 am to get a hot shower.

That's about all I need to know to survive camp. I could care less about hooking up with a boy, so that takes me out of the competition with my bunk mates for guys. Everything else is usually pretty chill.

But this year, as the week begins, I feel a storm brewing. It is not anything at camp. It is a storm exploding from inside me. The feelings have been unruly this year, seeping out of the boxes I have pushed them into. And this week, with the downtime, I feel the feelings from all the violent sexual trauma colliding, crashing into my day life, bringing significant disruption to my usual vacation flow.

I still swim the lake every day and live for the nights by the campfire roasting marshmallows, but in between, I am fixated on finding a way out, a way forward.

For the last two years, I have been searching for a way forward. In my sophomore year, I did 3 speeches and a short story on runaways. It was my way to see if that was a viable solution. I learned it was not. In my research, I found that I would likely be running into what I was trying to find a way out of, as many teens who run away end up being trafficked.

As I began to understand that all this was not normal, not just my place as a girl in the world or what men do to women and girls, I considered the option of telling someone if I could get it out of my mouth. But I had two friends, sisters, who did that. They spoke out about their dad and brother sexually abusing them, and that did not end well for them.

They ended up spinning out in foster care. That did not at all seem like a good forward for them. And many people around them that we both knew didn't believe them at all, and their dad was a nobody and a drunk. My dad was a community leader, a pastor, and a Kiwanis, and everyone loved him. What chance did I have of being believed? So, I shut down that path before it began.

The path I had been stuck on since that boy killed himself a year ago was self-harm, suicide. In one way it fights against my drive to survive, but it also is a way to take control of how I end. And I am having a hard time finding any other way out of the hardcore porn world, which is only getting worse and worse.

I am not sure I can survive much more of the extreme sexual and physical trauma they are dishing out. That last shoot crossed a line even for me. It referenced that day of my dad sticking a knife in me, but it felt like they took it much further. They did not have that boundary of needing to maintain an image. The only thing directing their actions was a sense of sadistic sexual satisfaction that they were willing to take as far as they needed to for their orgasm.

That sets off sirens and flashing red lights, indicating to me an off-the-charts danger that I did not know I was caught in. Almost like the night I saw my first porn film in the screening room, I felt a shattering light breaking in again. The perceived limits in my mind have helped me survive emotionally, but if there are no limits, then the danger is incalculable.

And if this really is a fight to the death, then maybe me beating them to the punch is a way of winning the game. At least I would choose how and when. Still, I am not sure. I don't like feeling cornered, but I also acknowledge that I may be cornered against the ropes without a workaround.

As I am wrestling with all this, the topic of suicide comes up at camp. And still looking for a different way forward, I approach the leader speaking about it. We talk for a while, but I don't really bring up my own suicidal thoughts. However, she hears the pill bottle I have in my pocket and asks me. I am honest about my suicidal thoughts but not about why I am suicidal. She is kind and encouraging, and the conversation ends well.

But the next day, I learn my parents will be told everything and that sets off new sirens and alarms inside me. I know my pretend family is not ready for that truth. I did learn an important lesson that day, though. I learned that as a minor, you are without privacy rights if you tell an adult something. Even when your parents are the source of harm, they will be told what you tell adults.

When I return home, I lie because that is what is expected of me in our daily performance as a family. I tell them it is about hating school, and they are satisfied with that. So after a brief interlude where Mom has her emotional breakdown at the stress of it all and Dad re-exerts his control over me, we all return to our normal.

And I try to both anticipate and brace for whatever is coming next for me on the porn set.

20. INTO THE SHADOW

Porn films are not really known for their dialogue, and my films are mostly just punctuated by one-liners that they feed me on the spot. They do not want me to read their script or their shoot plans. They liked to keep me in the dark because they preferred my natural reactions, my actual pain and terror, to my acting.

I am a fighter, and that has got me through as I walk night after night into unknown dangers. But our last shoot was a crushing moment for me in this fight. I had assumed there were still some humane lines they would not cross. I was wrong.

Knowing the boundaries of each circumstance and person in my life is what has kept me alive so far. I know that my father's image is the boundary that keeps him in check. He has the capacity to kill me, but his need to maintain his good-guy image keeps him from carrying it out. At the brothel, I knew that no matter how violent a man was, I just had to survive until that door opened again, and I heard the guard say, "Times up."

The boundaries in porn have been wide open from the start, and they seemed to just keep expanding beyond even my hypervigilant, sky-is-falling expectations.

The party orgy scenes expanded my expectation of having sex with one guy at a time. When being in that oblivion of sex from all sides normalized within me, then the boundaries expanded again. This time to me, at the center of the film in a series of aggressive gang rapes even staged in what appeared to be public settings. I don't think those scenes ever normalized within me, but I did begin to think they represented a normal sexual trauma present in the world around me.

The last boundary expansion was a return to the sexual torture of my childhood, but it went miles beyond what even my father could have envisioned or acted out. What I experienced that night was a porn form of female genital mutilation. They even had the doctor sew me up tight so that every time a man pulled out of me after that, it would hurt, and I would remember that moment. Until that night, I did not know that all this was within the boundaries of this corner of the hardcore porn world.

Maybe I was looking for boundaries in this corner of the porn world that did not exist to convince myself I could win this fight. Maybe in this arena, there are no rules, refs or scores. Maybe this is not about winning at all. I see now that this is a no-holds-barred, anything-goes kind of fight.

Maybe this is a fight to the death. That thought sends chills down my spine.

<u>Cue music:</u> Enter Sandman by Metallica plays its musical version of the entrance of the villain or the Death Star (Star Wars Series 1977) appearing on the horizon in my life.

As I walk from makeup onto the set the next night at the studio, I see possibly the tackiest porn set of all time. It has a noir look to it, mostly black, with a big velvet scar. Perhaps this is to indicate symbolically that it is curtains time for me. Perhaps it is a reference to porn films of the past.

Strobing light and loud, dissonantly tense music fills the air. If I were watching this movie, I would close my eyes now, sensing the terror ahead. But I am unable to flee from the scene I am walking into. So I disconnect and become steel inside instead.

The first man walks into the room and unties the scarlet cord from the curtain. Sensing the danger, I back up as if there is a way out, but there is not. He grabs me by the hair, pushes me down on the bed, and thrusts himself inside me while simultaneously wrapping the scarlet cord tight around my neck and beginning to constrict it as tight as he can.

I scan his eyes, trying to discern if he has it in him to kill me. I only see exhilaration, which cannot be a good sign. As I feel myself slipping into a shadowy world of death, I struggle harder, but he is a big man who is still on top of me. I started blacking out. It is as if I can hear the death birds, crows and vultures circling, waiting for my final breath. But then the shadowy scene gives way to another brighter scene. It is an open plain, like a savannah in Africa, maybe, and it is full of light. I breathe deeply in the peace and beauty of the world around me.

And then suddenly, I am gasping for air alone on the bed, back in the tackiest porn set ever. Alive but exhausted, I shut my eyes to recover. I can still feel the rope burn on my neck.

They stopped short of killing me. That may mean there is a boundary there, or they just want more scenes out of me. I can't be sure yet.

That place I went beyond the shadow world was like breathing in light for a second. It is the first time in a long time that I have felt that kind of beautiful world near me. I wonder what that was.

I hope that this will be my only experience with snuff scenes, but I am savvy enough to expect that there is more to come.

In the next scene, I feel my head thrust underwater, and my eyes shoot wide open to see a blurry, raging man with a full brown beard. I feel him thrust himself inside me repeatedly while he holds me under. I hold on for as long as I can. I fade into the shadow again and then move beyond back into the wide-open skies over the savannah. I feel scared passing through the shadow, but no fear at all in the light-filled land of the vast savannah and its wide open skies.

I am jolted back by my own choking and spewing of water onto the bathroom floor of this crappy apartment set in the porn studio. Maybe it is the loss of air each time, but I collapse in exhaustion each time after I realize I am alive and still breathing.

In the next scene, I am back on the first bed in different attire, if you can call it that, and the tacky velvet curtains are gone. I am looking up where the ceiling should have been, but there is only dark, empty space.

The building was converted from a huge ship repair dock into a porn studio, so the building ceilings are very high, but the sets often have their own ceilings. Evidently, the ceiling isn't important to this scene.

Cue music: Let Me Fall from Quidam (Cirque Du Soleil 1996), the sorrowful mystical music with a tinge of their French Canadian homeland, sings of my growing exhaustion and fading will. The touch of death felt better than my life, so my will to fight is flickering.

Staring into the black empty space I see a white pillow descending towards my face. For a second, before it covers my face, I look at the man holding it. He seemed less angry in this scene than he has in the last few. He seems more cold than angry this time around, and that scares me. My father is always the most dangerous when he is ice, not fire.

I am more disconnected as he simultaneously smothers me and rises to orgasm inside me. He pulls the pillow back just enough so they can get the shot of my deadening eyes before I black out again.

The true terror of the victim mixed with the look of death in their eyes is the money shot in these near-snuff films.

I wake up in the cheaper-looking apartment set where the tub is. I am lying naked on the floor. It feels like a metaphor for something. At the start, they at least pretended I was a rising star. Now, my star seemed to be falling, fading, but into what?

My head is full of cotton balls. I am delirious, and I cannot quite focus…that is, until I see the plastic bag in his hands. Immediately, my senses sharpen. I know exactly where this was headed. I start to move, but I am too late, and he is too muscular, well built. He flips me over like I am nothing and binds my hands. Planting his knee across me, he duct tapes the plastic bag around my head and shifts to straddle me.

He is cold as ice in his effect as he thrusts himself inside me. He is focused intently on my eyes. His blurring face looks orgasmic from my terror. And that is the last thing I see as I fade into the shadowy blackness.

Cue music: Bring Me to Life by Evanescence sings me through this shadow into whatever that wide open space beyond it is, restoring my connection to life, to my will to fight, to live.

When, into shadow, you feel yourself slipping
Revoke the bowed eyes, the shattered mirror skews and views
And through shadow and fire - Arise.
- Jewell Baraka

I am moving faster through the shadow each time, flippantly waving at the death birds circling as I move into the land of wide-open skies. In that place, I can breathe again. It feels warm, not like the dark coldness of the set or of my life. It is life-giving, like warm sunlight and fresh air.

And then I am back on that crappy apartment bathroom floor in the porn studio, gasping for air, ripping the bag open with my hands that are now cut free. From outside the room, I hear just one line spoken: "Man, that bitch won't die." "Cut"

The scene may have come out looking erotic, but inside my story, behind my eyes, it is a flatline on the sexually erotic scale. There is nothing erotic about being choked, strangled, suffocated, smothered, or drowned while being raped.

In this film, the look of terror and death in my eyes is the money shot, the moment that men craving a lethal mix of power and sex will get off on.

That experience of being taken to the edge of death for the sake of sexual gratification is a mind fuck in a deep way. Seeing that kind of hate or indifference that would kill a human or come right to the edge of it for the sake of a better orgasm is touching pure psychosis, and that changes you. And I say that as a girl who grew up with a psychopath, a girl who stopped being naive at age 7.

A dark tunnel of pain has opened and is expanding within me. Death feels like a shadow lingering near me, waiting for the right moment to snatch me from this Earth.

But simultaneously, I feel the light from those moments beyond the shadow. And in that touch, there is life and strength. Beyond the shadow, I felt wide open skies full of light flooding into me like oxygen, refilling my strength for the fight yet to come.

21. THE FINAL FACE-OFF

There is more than one way to win a fight. You can use brute force, technique, taunting or you can take out their heart and will. They had already violently violated, beaten me, tortured me, and humiliated me. And yet, there was still a spark of life within me as long as I knew that I was not the source of harm.

Predators, oppressors, and abusers have a way of finding weaknesses. Like sharks or vampires, they sense blood nearby and circle in on it. John planned his shoots from this kind of instinct. So whether or not he knew about me, I believe, on some level, he sensed my need to not be the source of harm and wrote his script accordingly.

The night seemed off, different from the start. Since my first night on the set three years ago, they had always "dressed" me in cherry red. I was Candy Cane or Candy Cunt. They went back and forth, but in either case, they saw cherry red as my color. But tonight, they put me in black leather and metal.

This sets off loud alarms and sirens within me. In a world where there are not many things that remain the same from night to night, the color red has been one constant for me. My long history of experience with traumatic environments has taught me that every change, no matter how small, is important. Any kid that comes out of trauma will tell you that.

So, the switch of color tonight has left me seeing red, ironically, with all of my nerve endings standing up in hypervigilant focus. My crimson red lips against my pale white face are the only visible remnant of red on me tonight.

At the makeup powder cloud, I realize my time has expired. No more analysis; time to put up the internal face shield of bravado and just react. I do not know what is coming, but I will have to figure out how to fight as it happens. The fight is now just waiting to hear "action" to begin.

As I walk onto the set, I scan and process everything as quickly and precisely as I can, as if I am some Android from a sci-fi movie.

They changed the set. I expected that. It is wide open, 3 times the size of a normal set. For once, I feel the true immensity and vacuous emptiness of the porn studio itself.

There is a line of naked young men bound, their mouths taped, standing in front of a huge movie screen. This baffles me. Usually, I am the one bound, chained, whipped, stripped. What does this mean?

John moves out of the shadows he often directs from and into the obnoxious strobe light. He looks into my eyes and smirks at me, his version of a smile, nodding to the soundman on his left. Loud metal music begins playing. "Action!" he yells as he walks back to his chair.

<u>Cue music:</u> Power by KMFDM, fueled by a pulsing industrial vibe, surges through me, reflecting the shift of positioning and atmosphere happening both inside and outside of me at this moment.

Immediately, images start flashing across the huge screen behind the line of men. It is a highlight reel of the last 3 years. The metal-scraping cacophony of my gang rapes, beatings, torture sessions, stranglings and asphyxiations are all there in strobing snippets before me.

It is an armor-piercing nightmarish; this is your life montage of every: pounding pain, shattering darkness, world imploding, equilibrium failing, drowning in pain, and scarlet skin-covered moment. Surges of everything at once rush through me.

While I am mesmerized by the screen, someone slips a whip into my right hand and a knife into my left hand. John steps forward just enough so I can see him and nods his head towards the men lined up before me. As the rage surges within me, suddenly, I understand what he wants me to do. He wants me to become the villain, to take all my hurt and rage and become the one inflicting the pain on these men before me.

Years of sexual violation and violence mean the well of rage within me is deep and full, and he is pushing on that, pushing on me to release it all in one blow.

Propelled forward by surging emotion and rage, I scream and crack the whip again and again and again. It feels good to have power. It feels strong and peaceful somehow.

So I crack the whip more. I am riding a wave of rage and frenzy as I move towards the men before me. I notice the knife in my left hand. I move in closer, propelled forward by this force of rage I have long subverted within me. Turning my rage outward taps into that rushing headlong force that I had first six years ago at the tree, the night of my first gang rape and entrance into the world of commercial sex.

But in the midst of moving forward to strike I lock eyes with one of the young men. And I see in his eyes the fear and shame that I have often felt in my own eyes. Instantly, the force of rage lurches to a stop within me because I know he is not any of my oppressors. He is just a young man being abused and possibly trafficked like me.

I fall to my knees, dropping the knife and whip, crying out loudly in pain at what I have nearly done, at what I am becoming. To harm, to become one who harms others like a man after man in my life, is the worst thing I could ever be, and I nearly crossed that line.

My eyes are closed. The surging rage has lurched to a stop, but the reverberations of it all are still running through me. I feel a peace come over me and even the set around me feels still. Maybe they never anticipated that I would not conform to their plan and are trying to understand what is happening.

It feels like long minutes, but maybe it is just seconds, really. For me, internally, it is another moment of shattering light where I remember who I want to be, and I am lost in it. When I open my eyes in the strobing light, everyone is staring at me as if something about me has locked them into a place where they are.

I stare back, looking from person to person around the room. After a few seconds, it is as if they all unfreeze. Everyone starts moving, but no one is setting up for a reshoot. Instead, everyone starts cleaning up for the night.

They all seem a little baffled by what has just happened. There is something about me they do not understand. They are used to people falling in line with their script. And I have done that plenty of times in the past three years, but not tonight.

22. WHO WILL DEFINE WHO I WILL BE?

I survived the night; my core self or soul or essence remains. I feel a flicker of flame still inside me. It feels like a victory in the fight for who I will become.

But all the surging rage has not returned to its locked box within me. It seems to be seeking an object to focus its attention on. And if I cannot harm others that only leaves myself as a focus for the rage. And I did see myself come right to the edge of harming last night, and that feels like a betrayal of who I have always wanted to be or become.

The released, now unboxed rage is becoming a dark undertow pulling me under. This flow of rage that has been tapped into will not be easily reversed. And having no emotional tools or healthy releases, the rage keeps focusing on the one person I have been raised to blame: myself. Suddenly, all the residual rage is pointing like a gun at my own face.

I have been depressed, understandably, for a couple of years. I have been struggling with suicidal thoughts and informal plans for about a year. Now I feel a drive, an urgency, behind those plans.

<u>Cue music:</u> Dead Souls by Nine Inch Nails chilling industrial vibe reflects in me all that I feel in this shadow: the shadow I passed through in the snuff shoots and the shadow of failure to become a better version of myself that I had just experienced in immersion into my own rage, rage powerful enough to cause harm.

I want to go back to the savannah with the warm light and fresh air to breathe it in, but I don't know how to find it again. Maybe I will find it again in death if I have the strength to carry it out.

Suddenly, every day feels heavy, like I am walking against the tide's pull. Every violent sexual act has built a well of rage within me that is now turning against me.

<u>Cue music:</u> Breathe Me by Sia, fills my atmosphere. The deeply reflective, introspective serenade lulls me into a much-needed calm after all this upheaval of emotion.

> *I am dangling from the edge of a cliff*
> *Above a bottomless ravine.*
> *Fighting to hold on*
> *But my grip is slipping*
> *And the cliff's edge*
> *Is crumbling*
> *Through my hands.*
> **- Jewell Baraka**

Consumed by this flow of rage against myself, which is actually an internalization of all the violence against me, I swallow a bottle of pills. Waves of anxiety and peace fluctuate as I swallow the pills on the floor of my high school bathroom. From anxiety to peace, back and forth, I move until, finally, the drowsiness takes over.

I move back into consciousness to the sound of an ambulance screaming. And then back into the deep sleep. A day or two later I awaken to the sound of my heart monitor beeping.

I have failed. I am terrified of the chain of events I have just set off. I did not plan to live, so I have no idea what will happen now. In trying to end my life, I have spoken my truth for the first time, and the world around me is not ready for that.

My suicide attempt was my first real act of speaking my truth. I screamed the excruciating pain and rage of sexual trauma and the fallout from that as I swallowed pill after pill. I was able to speak my truth in that moment only because I thought I would never have to face the consequences.

It is dangerous to speak the truth when you are still in an unsafe place. Every abused, raped, trafficked, or sexually exploited person knows that.

Now face to face with consequences, I had to figure out quickly how to silence my speaking, the scream I had just released into the world.

The social worker circling my room tries to get me to speak, but I know the moment for speaking has passed. Stuffing every bit of the truth I can back into my mouth is the only way to mediate the damage now.

I lie to appease the anger that I know will soon be escalating off the charts, for truth cannot be spoken without consequence in systems of abuse and oppression. "I just hate high school and couldn't stand it one more minute," I say over and over again. "No, of course, it has nothing to do with my family." Lie after lie, just trying to silence the truth I have spoken.

They refer me to a teen mental health unit of the hospital. I am grateful for the delay before I have to return to life under my father's skies, but unsure of what to expect from this new culture and group of peers.

<u>Cue music:</u> Bleed Like Me by Garbage, an edgy rock commentary, fits the questions I have about this moment well.

The teen mental health unit on the 9th floor of the hospital is strange, though more normal than I expect it to be. It is more of a crisis stabilization space than it is a long-term space and it is not for adults. No one is talking to themselves or acting out any of the more extreme disorders or behaviors I have seen in movies. Mostly, it is people who have attempted suicide, experienced abuse, have eating disorders, and a few who were placed here for anger control issues.

But whatever our labels, we are just teenagers trying to survive our dangerous worlds. We sense this in each other and form connections, alliances even. We trust each other more than any adult there, but that doesn't mean we talk about the deep things. We don't.

Mandy and I bond over food. She likes the healthy salads they are giving me, and I like the more highly caloric meals that they are giving her, so we trade every meal. We are both very happy with our trade. We were just kids trying to figure out how to get what we wanted in a strange space.

Only years later did I realize that Mandy was being treated for an eating disorder and that I had inadvertently hindered her on her own path forward.

My roommate Diamond adopted the 70s as her musical genre; maybe it is the acid trips she describes that make her so fond of Pink Floyd. She plays them on repeat incessantly. They are not really my thing, but they do sing about pain in a trance-like way that resonates with my present experience.

I like her, but I realize I can't trust her when I find out she is informing on me. She tells the staff about the things I cut myself with in exchange for privileges. She is there for anger issues and has a need to control everything, including me. But there is little chance of that as I am deep in my turtle shell at the moment where no one can reach me.

Matt brings me the most eventful moment of my stay when he decides he can't sit still a moment longer and tries to escape through the ceiling, which he subsequently falls back through while he is still in the unit. But he is so surprised by his fall that he bolts, hitting the locked doors at full tilt and knocking them open. Alarms sound, and hospital staff that look unused to sprinting jump into action in a hilarious-looking chase, ending in a tackle and his safe return to the unit.

The moment is the topic of discussion for days, perhaps even years, since it made it to my pages here.

During our free time, we bond over our war stories. We are not expressing the deeper trauma, just the surface trauma of high school and our united belief in the nonspecific stupidity of adults that we are able to speak. Still, as we connect, we see humanity and the sincere struggle to survive in each other's eyes and something deeper happens. We silently realize we can't all be wrong or to blame for whatever landed us here.

As individuals, we are often gaslighted by the broken people around us, but together, it is hard not to see that it cannot all be on us. We cannot possibly be the sole cause of all this brokenness we have jointly experienced.

I hear in their stories that there are other people to blame for their pain. This ignites a faint spark within me. Maybe, just maybe, I am not completely to blame either.

I am deep in my turtle shell, but I take in everything. There is a window seat in my room. I sit there as much as possible, looking out over the city, running things over in my mind. I especially like to see the city at night, the lights smeared impressionistically by the Portland rain. One night, as I am looking out into the smeared city lights, I feel something I do not recognize.

My emotional vocabulary is nearly non-existent as emotions are human, and humanity is not generally allowed for me. But the feelings have been starting to emerge despite my perceived inhumanity.

The feeling emerging tonight is safety, but it is such an uncommon feeling for me that I do not immediately recognize it. I feel it deeply for a split second, and it changes me. It gives me something ahead to move towards.

It reminds me that safety can exist for me. If safety exists here, then maybe it can exist in other worlds outside of this one. Maybe there are skies beyond these rain-filled, stormy skies where I could be safe. I just have to find out where there are safer skies for me.

Despite the spark of light, I stay in my shell. I am under no delusions that I have reached that alternate universe just because I felt a spark. Now is not the time to reach, speak, or jump. I know without a doubt that my housing is temporary, and I am still under the dangerous skies of my father.

As if on cue, my father comes to visit me at the hospital. He doesn't come because he cares. He does not feel much of anything, but he has a performance to carry out. If he comes, he can tell everyone that he came and gather their acclaim for him as a benevolent man and father. That's the spin he will weave it into.

In reality, he is furious that I have spoken the truth of my reality in my suicide attempt, and he comes to reassert control. He tells me, "Satan is using you to be an embarrassment to me and the church."

Of course, this is all about his precious image. How had I missed that?!

I see the poisonous duplicity of his words, and yet the poison in them still creates its intended trauma. I stomp off, fuming, all the way to the smashball court, which is two rooms away.

Smashball is a game close to pickleball, but it is played inside, and the rules allow you to bounce the ball off the ceiling, thus the name: Smashball. I smash the hell out of the smashball, imagining his face on each ball.

Shortly after my father comes to visit me, he stages a violent overthrow to seize back control. He is done waiting, so he makes his power play and orders the doctors to release me. I am safer in the hospital, which also means that I am less suicidal while I am there. So, unable to get a "two doctor hold" to prevent my removal, they are overthrown by my father.

And I am returned to life under his brutal skies.

23. THE FINAL SCENE

Home is a shit show, more than usual when I get back from the hospital. I am back in my father's domain, one of the kingdoms he rules over. And he is in a rage, furious that I have marred his image and the family's by attempting suicide.

The community church he pastors is his other power place. And he feels dishonored there and possibly endangered by my clear statement of dissatisfaction with my life. But he need not have worried about their response. They are all rallying around him in a time of need created by this "rebellious child" of his. He has indoctrinated them into belief in his unquestionable goodness and our flawed natures exceptionally well.

I have violated the golden rule of every mafia movie and our family: "Betray the family and die." But lucky for me, with all these eyes on him, he cannot kill me, but that does not stop him from expressing his extreme displeasure at my actions. Angry reprisals, verbal, physical, and sexual, are normal in my first few weeks home.

I have had a couple of months to just focus on this single fight. It feels disorienting. I am used to fighting many bouts at once.

I am not sure what the pause is about on the porn side. Maybe my suicide attempt they are counting as a win, or maybe it weirds them out. My last night in the porn studio ended so strangely, and I have no idea how they processed that night. Maybe they think I am nuts. Wouldn't that be ironic?!

But right then on cue, as if they can hear me wondering, they come for me again. I have no idea what to expect or ideal of how this night might play out. I replay the last night at the studio in my mind all the way there.

My refusal to conform to their script surprised even me that last night we filmed. But I am under no delusion that somehow I have gained their respect from not falling in line with their script. After three years in porn, three years in prostitution, and 17 years with my father, I am not naive. I know that refusals are always punished. So I shake violently all the way to the studio.

Despite being out of practice as the trunk opens and the streetlight hits my face, my mask of bravado automatically clicks back into place. I emerge from the car and walk towards the studio as if I am choosing whatever storyline is waiting for me there.

Just through the studio warehouse door, I feel someone grab my arm and nearly jump out of my skin. "Ready, Candy," I hear, just as I have hundreds of nights before. It is Greta, my handler. I take a quick breath and as I quickly regain my steely exterior.

After a quick run through hair and makeup, I am taken to the set. It looks like a medieval city with a stone wall around it. There is a huge gate between the inner city and the road that leads to the world outside of the city.

<u>Cue music:</u> Walk This Earth Alone by Lauren Christy releases its melodic, angsty, slightly haunting refrain into me as I face forward and walk into the set again, like I always do, alone.

Trauma
Wrapped around every vital part
Constricting,
Compressing
Like an internal tourniquet
Restricting blood flow
An instrument of contested asphyxiation

> *Driving my eyes*
> *Into hypervigilant focus.*
> **- Jewell Baraka**

There is one difference tonight, though. The hospital has given me hope of a possible life ahead in another place where I may not be alone anymore.

I walk aggressively through the open gate inside the city walls. My gaze sharpens. I focus intently as I see everyone there waiting for me. If I have learned anything from all my trauma, it is to always size up the situation and person in front of you.

My eyes scan the room as I walk into the center of the set. I am expecting to find rage, but instead, I sense indifferent disconnection. This is new, but I don't have time to process it because right then, I hear "Action."

And with that, a whole crowd of men descend upon me, dragging me outside the city walls. From there, it feels like a fairly normal night on the porn set. Sexual violence through gang rape and physical beatings has become the norm for me in the last 3 years, and this last night is no different.

The theme of the scene is reminiscent of old samurai movies where they cast a warrior out of the city to wander the world alone but with more raping. It seems to go on for a long time, and it is brutal but less than some of the nights that have come before. And eventually, it does end.

John, who likes to throw in one-liners at the end of each scene, says somewhat poetically for him, "Done with this bitch, on to the next one."

That is the last line I ever hear come out of his mouth. And with the sight of his back walking away from me, Candy is officially written out. After that night, they never came for me again.

For the last year, I had increasingly seen the end of my trafficking in porn in my death. So many nights, in a metaphoric and literal sense, I have seen death waiting for me, circling me like a shadowy character in my story.

Poe had a raven. Frodo had the Nazgul. Neo fought against Agent Smith.

My opponent of physical death is conquered, and yet my survival in other fights still hangs in the balance. "Raging against the dying of the light" is an existential war waged in the physical, emotional, spiritual, and relational realms all at once. And it is not clear yet where I stand in each bout.

I am in shock. It is hard to take in that these last three years of nuclear bombs being dropped on my life may have just ended. Have I really filmed the very last scene I ever will for them?

I go to all my favorite perches and write, processing this development to try, trying to work out where I am and what will happen next. I circle through the questions of what this means for me. Am I free or being thrown away? Does it matter? Did I win, or did they win, or was this always a no-win scenario?

I feel both freedom and rejection. The pattern of being rejected and cast out is strong in my life. And I feel the echoes of the last porn scene we shot.

Hardcore porn is an upside-down world that I never wanted to belong to, but for a while, in a twisted way, I had. So, as it ends, I feel a strange sense of loss and rejection. And I cannot help but wonder what it means about me that even the worst world I have ever been submerged in has rejected me in the end.

But I also feel a new, rising sense of freedom running through me. And night after night, as I do not hear the car approach, I feel a surreal, slowly evolving sense of warm sunlight and fresh air growing within me for the first time in a very long time.

This is not the end of the action movie I saw in my mind so many times for myself. It is not that moment when all my perpetrators are dead on the floor, and the studio explodes into a flaming inferno as I turn and walk away from it.

Real life is infinitely more complex than the black-and-white conquering endings of action movies. But I have chosen not to harm, and so the lack of explosions or dead bodies at the porn studio for me is actually a win on the level of all my action movie endings and heroes.

24. MY FIRST FREEDOM MOMENT

<u>Cue music:</u> It's My Life by No Doubt releases its bouncing, ska-vibed independence declaration into the world in and around me as I revel in my moment of freedom.

This new freedom breaks forth in the Spring of my senior year, and for once, I am able to savor life as just a 17-year-old. With all the celebrations around graduation, it feels as if the whole world is celebrating my freedom with me. Of course, no one knows what I have just escaped, but I have escaped, and it is a time to celebrate…so I do.

I am celebrating something very different from my classmates, but they do not know that. On the outside, I look like a normal teen excited to be almost free of high school.

It is fortunate for me that my first freedom moment coincides with a moment of freedom happening in the world around me. For once, I am on the same page as my peers. Usually, our lives feel so different.

While I was trying to continue breathing, they were often worried about popularity or boys. Boys were the last thing I needed. The storyline between me and the male gender has been sexually violent from the start. Desiring boys in that context would be equivalent to self-harm for me.

Self-harm patterns are strong in me, but somehow, I am smart enough not to pursue further harm at the hands of boys. I have enough men to handle already. I cannot overcome all my patterns of self-harm at once, but at least I can escape this one context of self-harm.

The sexual trauma weighs on me, ages me, and fills me with concerns that are atypical as far as I know in the people around me. My trauma has made it impossible for me to be a normal kid or teen. But with this heavy weight lifted from me, I can try out being a normal teen like them for a few months. For once, we are in sync, with no reference to the band intended.

The divisions of popularity are falling away these last few months of our senior year as everything is about to shift. Nostalgia is high even among those who hated each other during school, and a sense of rising freedom and unity is pervasive among us. It is a moment where the past seems better than it was, and the future seems brighter than it probably is, but nobody cares because it is a time of celebration and reveling.

I jump into every graduation event as if this is the only life I have been living all along. For once, there is a glimmer of light ahead of me. I cruise the streets in cars with friends, listening to music. I go to all the parties and celebrations and invite people to graduation.

I even go to the school-sponsored after-party and win a mirror, which is ironic on one hand since I have always hated mirrors, but maybe it is a sign of healing to come. I hope that my shattered internal mirror will one day heal.

Flash Forward: It will, but it will be a fight, the main card fight of my healing. Throughout the years of healing that follow, I write about the #NewDayRising. The new day rises for me not in a moment but in pieces of the dawn that I receive one at a time.

And this freedom moment is the first piece I receive of the new day rising for me.

<u>Cue music:</u> Feeling Good by Nina Simone. The soulful fight song heralds the first glimpse of a rising new day for me.

Morning-hued rising light
Sharpening forms
Clearing off of
Groggy fog banks
On my soul's shores.

25. FINAL ESCAPE

As summer ends and my classmates go away to school, I begin planning my final escape.

My father has denied me going away to school, citing the suicide attempt as his reason, though it has more to do with his control than care. It is a power play. He senses he is losing control of me, and he is fighting to regain that control. I hold the truth about him inside me, even if I am not yet speaking it, and nothing scares him more than that.

After my suicide attempt, the hospital mandated counseling. This has been a gift for me but a threat to him. Counseling is opening up a new world to me, the world of my humanity. Before this, outside of poems, I had no grid to understand, let alone express my own emotions. I rarely express my emotions interpersonally because there is no room for my humanity amidst the worlds of abuse and exploitation that I move between.

Violet, my counselor, is the first voice I have really heard from outside my family and the first one who does not care who my father is. She only cares about helping me. She does her job well and never crosses any boundaries into personalization that she shouldn't. I have not really had parents, so I want her to be one, but she knows that isn't her place. And I am beginning to accept that as well.

It is hard to understand, but I am glad she maintains her boundaries because if she became my mother, I might never leave, and I know that is what I need most. Even without that deeper connection, she is teaching so much that I count her as my first real experience of being parented.

So with Violet on my side, free from my exploitation in porn, I begin plotting my escape from my father and the land I have survived. Plotting is necessary because the best way to beat a psychopath is to somehow hide that you are fighting them. You have to outthink them and devise a plan that they falsely believe is their own. You have to give them the illusion of control.

For my father, the chess move, the solution is a Christian college where he personally knows a professor. This gives him the illusion of control because, in some sense, at least to this one professor, he will be known there.

The school is far away from him, but not far from the beach, which I have always wanted to live near. Still, I am conflicted about this solution because I don't really want to go to a Christian school. And also, there is the issue of the essay they require on their application about your relationship with Jesus. I have no idea what to say about that. We feel disconnected at this evolution of my life.

It is not that I am not personally spiritual. I am, but it has all become a dense fog bank that is hard to see into. I am not sure where I stand on anything at the moment. And I know that I do not fit the shiny, happy Christian girl box the school will want me to portray in this essay. So, I am conflicted at best about this solution.

But wise as always, Violet says to me, "If I were you and I had the opportunity to get a 1000+ miles away from here, I would do whatever it takes to make that happen." So, I decide that despite all my reservations, I will fully commit to getting into this school.

My essay is a pure work of fiction, but it gets me in and away from both my father and the land of my exploitation, and that is all that matters.

This year of counseling after my suicide attempt has been essential. It has helped me stabilize and begin to learn the emotional truths of my own humanity that have been hidden from me. But there is only so much you can heal when you are still in an unsafe place.

Now it is time to go, to finally break free from the oppressive, abusive regime of my father.

I planned my escape on a midnight bus many times when I was 15. I literally was almost a runaway, but the reality that I would be running to people like the people I was running away kept me from ever taking that step.

My midnight bus has turned into a packed car driving 1000 miles away to school on the way into the second freedom moment of my life.

<u>Cue music:</u> Goodbye to You by Michelle Branch soundtracks my letting go of everything that came before mile by mile. I knew I would not go back.

Making decisions without regret and then never looking back or wavering is a gift I have. It helps me keep moving forward in my life. Still, in each transition, I have to intentionally let go of everything that came before. The road trip becomes that moment in this transition for me.

When it is over, and I am alone on the balcony of my 7th-floor dorm, grateful to be there, alive, watching the sunset in a new land. And in this moment I receive my second piece of the dawn rising for me.

It isn't the exact exit or location I imagined at age 15, 16 or 17, but I am near Los Angeles, the city I always envisioned running toward.

And big plus I am not on the streets of Hollywood or under the Santa Monica Pier where I had imagined I might end up at 15.

There is no fear here of how I will find my next meal or where I will sleep. And I need that safety and stability as I begin my healing. Despite the extreme trauma in porn, I am grateful every day that I did not run away when I was 15.

Welcome week feels like a celebration of the new life that is beginning for me. Freedom and glimmers of light are being released into my life.

The raging darkness
Slips silently into the day
As if it were the most natural of things.
And this breach of my soul
Slowly seals as I watch
Chaos fading to peace.
- Jewell Baraka

26. ON THE BEACH

The Earth beneath me shakes still
From yesterday's emotive tectonic shift
Nausea hits me in waves
And then wanes.
The Earth's shift is done
But the aftershocks
Within me shakes still.
Paradigms in double exposure
Strove violently
In a cosmic bout
As the old fights to maintain its hold
And the new steps up...to take its rightful place.
*- **Jewell Baraka***

It has been a year since I arrived at my new home in Southern California. Sun streaming down on my face, I am sitting on the beach by the pier on a Sunday morning, watching the surfers with a coffee in my right hand and a slice of pizza in my left. Odd combo I know, but it is me at the moment.

All year, the reality that I was physically safe has been settling in. The surreal feeling still comes in and out. I fought so hard all my life it is hard to believe I have really survived. So much of life was a nightmare that when it wasn't any longer, it seemed surreal, like a dream too good to be real, which is not to say that my life had become a Hallmark movie.

The other reason it feels surreal is that all the battles within me connected to my past trauma remain between me and a healed life.

Following my successful title fight for my continued breathing and physical freedom, I needed a break. I needed to just breathe for a time amidst managing the fallout from all that came before.

That is all I have really done this first year free: manage the fallout, which has been extensive and breathe. That is more than enough.

There is a storm of emotional fallout that happens when you are finally physically safe, and I am right in the middle of that. But the suicidal ideation has retreated because every bit of the flooding trauma, migraines, and emotions reminds me that I am indeed alive. And having survived, why would I kill myself now?

Suicide, for me, was always a way to take control of my fate. In the fixed game of sexual trauma, it was a way to take my end out of their hands. But once that imminent threat was gone, I did not have a need for that control mechanism anymore. In the fallout of the trauma, of course, I still have suicidal thoughts, but there is no real drive behind them anymore.

I have not suddenly shape-shifted into a superhero or a perfect life. A year out, I am still cutting, and patterns of self-harm run through me, but I am harming less and breathing more. The self-harm that continues is about blame and shame, not death. And I am learning in counseling to communicate my trauma in ways other than self-harm.

I am believing more every day that I have, in fact, survived. Of course, there are many bouts for inner survival that still remain ahead of me. But even in those, there are sparks of light, hope of the healing to come.

<u>Cue music:</u> Today by Lauren Christy asserting with the perfect singer songwriter edge, the attitude that fits this new day of healing in my life.

Flames flicker
Fusing my eyes, my shattered sight.
Flames shoot up
Burning off death's many masks
Flames explode
In a funeral pyre of healing fire
Igniting
What will be in me
A blazing bonfire of life.
- Jewell Baraka

Deep resonations of gratitude for the unexpected gift of my continued breathing on this planet wake me up every day. I know this kind of gift asks for a response. The only response I see before me is continuing the fight to become the better version of myself, to fulfill the vow that I made there on the porn theater floor when I was 14.

To become a better version of myself, I will have to face the pain, shame and shadows of all my past trauma, abuse, trafficking, and exploitation. I am no more than a few minutes into the first round of that fight yet, but I will continue the fight.

This year has been about breathing and managing the erratic flow of emotions, which is the fallout from finally being physically safe and defense mechanisms releasing their hold. But also, it has been about navigating a new social culture around me.

I had always escaped the church I was raised in by immersion in public school culture and my friends there. I found my own music, culture and a diversity of people, and that's what I raised myself in. I understood Christian culture, but I always saw it as a hostile environment to survive. It was my dad's world, not mine.

Here, I am surrounded day and night by that culture, and it is familiar in one way, but it is also foreign and, at times, still feels hostile to me. My insides are exploding into my external reality, and the trauma that has been hidden inside for so long is now showing on the outside. That does not always go over well in this shiny, happy performance culture.

My first roommate asks me to take down the rock posters on my wall. It seems, in her mind, they reflect negatively on her. But I love my posters. So I kindly tell her that what I put on my wall has nothing to do with her. And defiantly, I leave them up.

<u>Cue music:</u> Fascination Street by the Cure plays their unique sound. I am trying to find my own unique sound and expression. They inspire me to search out my own expression and encourage me to be exactly who I am with all my quirks.

What I hate most in this foreign culture is the three days a week I am mandated to go to church; they call it chapel. And on top of that the social pressure demands I also go to church on Sunday. But I have just broken free of an oppressive regime I am not about to submit to another.

Begrudgingly I go to chapel, always hovering just below the most absences I can have and not get in trouble. But no social culture, no matter how strong, can force me to attend church on Sunday as well.

And that is how I ended up here at the beach by the pier on a Sunday. I am a fighter, but I have learned it is as important to know when to avoid a fight as it is to fight like hell when you have to. This is my workaround. I leave the dorms every Sunday between 9 and 12, during church hours, and go to the beach, where I watch surfers and eat pizza. And when I return, everyone just assumes that I have gone to church, and I do not correct them.

In a way, this is my church. I connect to the waves, sunlight, peace, and chill vibes. Sitting on the ledge on Sunday morning with my coffee and slice of pizza, watching the surfers is probably the best church I have ever been to.

All year, I have been finding creative ways to live, heal, and rise into who I am meant to be. And I sense how vital each instance of free self-expression is in becoming myself inside and out. It is a time not to separate the inside and out but to finally allow it to begin to merge in this stage of my healing.

Growing up as the pastor's kid, I learned to "smile for the cameras" at church and in the community when I was performing the part of me in my father's world. But no more. I will never do that again. Even in this foreign culture, I am as much myself as I know and have strength for.

Cue music: Everlong by Foo Fighters rocks its rising theme of strength and another piece of the new day for the person I have been waiting for...me.

The once seared sky
Fused by lightning
Is healing
Reuniting the long
Separated halves
Of day and night

The war that
Once upon a nightmare
Tore them apart
Has ended.
And the winds of peace rush in
To reconcile their disputes
As night and day
Resolve to share my sky.

There has been one big surprise here. Though I am an anomaly in this culture, and most do not understand me, I have found one group that does. I am part of a support group on campus for girls who have been sexually abused. It is ahead of its time, especially in church culture, which is always slow to see abuse within its walls and power structures. My life is proof of that.

There are 15-20 of us in the group, and everyone here has an abuser who is a pastor, elder or man in good standing in their church. In each other's stories, we see that we are not alone and we are not the problem. Our abusers are the problem, along with the culture that protects them.

But change has begun. We are initiating change by speaking our stories, first to each other and safe people, maybe later to the perpetrators themselves, and finally to the world.

Speaking our stories is always where change can begin. When we speak our stories, it is an offer, an opportunity to acknowledge the truth and reach for transformation. What happens after that is not up to us. We speak our truth, and then, even if the perpetrators and the world around us deny it or refuse to change, we are free.

This group has also initiated the release of my voice into the world. I am writing a weekly anonymous column telling the story of my abuse and perspective, though not yet my trafficking, in the school newspaper. It is a small but important step on my way to using my voice to effect change.

<u>Cue music:</u> Daylight by Delirium projecting light-filled lyrics into my future, projecting the stars, moon, glimmers, glimpses and pieces of the dawn that will lead me through the shadows and tunnels of healing ahead into the light of a new day in my life.

Rays of sunlight
Beating down warmth
Easing the chill
Of a long dark night
In tunnels of inhuman hate
Healing strobing pain filled visions
Of my subterranean existence
In the once upon a nightmare that came before Restoring my plundered sense of self
In bursts of light and flickering film
Of what's to come.
The tunnels morphing into a chrysalis
The tight dark space giving way in breaths and bursts
Until...exploding through my shell
I open my eyes
Extend my multicolored phoenix wings wide
And rise.
- Jewell Baraka

The surfers, waves, and sand under my feet remind me that I have indeed survived and that there is life here for me.

Sitting on the beach, I feel my past, present, and future converge. The fire to write and speak and change the world around me has only just ignited, but somewhere inside, I feel the bonfire of transformation it may someday become.

And in the warmth of the sun shining down on my face, I feel the naked, shivering 14-year-old girl on the cold concrete porn studio floor begin to heal and rise in strength, skill, sense of self, and a clarity of voice.

"Sometimes in the fight, we find the warrior we always were."

Epilogue: Writing to Speak

Speaking our stories is as essential for the healing of our own sense of human value as it is for the reforming of the world around us. That said, what that process looks like in our lives is as diverse as we are. Our stories are connected but simultaneously unique, and the process and particular details of rising to speak our stories are best when they resemble us as individuals.

For me, rising to speak came first through writing and was constantly facilitated by writing as I rose to speak pieces of my story in more powerful ways and heal deeply as I did. I have an extroverted side to me, but I am definitely an introvert. Maybe that is why writing was such a breakthrough tool for me.

I was completely shut down and without emotional intelligence or language when my healing began. Speaking began as a part of healing me and my story. For me, it had to begin that way.

We often focus on healing the world through our stories, which is important and noble. Healing the world is certainly at the core of my intentions as I release my story into the world, but I am also clear on the place of this release within the longer process of rising to speak my story. For survivors, the healing we receive from writing, speaking, and sharing our story with safe people long before we are able to project it loudly into the world is vital.

In the post MeToo culture, I love that the walls of silence are falling, and it is stunning to hear voices speaking their stories courageously together. There are more walls that need to fall. Still, I worry that survivors conforming to a world pushing them may be blurting out their stories before they have done the work leading up to that moment and may not be able to weather the storm of social opinion and internal fallout that often follows.

Early on in my own process, I saw this dynamic played out in the self-harm awareness movement. Just as everyone began talking about cutting and self-harm, a couple of survivors emerged, told their stories, and became the faces of the movement. About a year later, it came out that one of them was still cutting. From their story, I learned that the spotlight is best when it comes further down the road of personal healing.

The deep dive into seeing and healing the abyss of my trauma was the way forward. Everyone has their own path that was mine.

For me, rising to speak my story began even before I was free and healing. It began that night when I was 14 in the porn studio screening room, where I vowed to survive to become a better version of myself. That intention was the foundation of the healing that led me here.

However, speaking my story out loud couldn't really begin while I was still unsafe and in the midst of my trauma. To survive my trauma, I had to live shut down and in a performance of my life to preserve my life. We often have to survive to get to a place where we are physically safe before we can even begin to truly speak the story we have to tell.

When I was 17, listening to the sound of my heart monitor in the ICU after I had tried to kill myself, I watched the social worker circling my room and knew that I needed to learn to speak my truth. Not being able to speak my truth in that moment pushed me to fight for that, so in another moment, further down the road, I would be able to speak when the opportunity arose.

Speaking my truth out loud started as the blurting of snippets and pieces of my story to licensed therapists who are trained to be non-judgmental, so they were a safe place to start speaking. None of them were old enough to be my parents, and they all maintained their professional boundaries of non-attachment well, but still, there was a dimension of that process that was like being parented for the first time. They received my truth in a welcoming way because they were strong enough to hold the trauma and wise enough to give me tools to help me hold and process the trauma well. They didn't have personal love to give me, but all the time and energy they poured into me was certainly its own form of love.

Friends, on the other hand, I learned had personal love and attachment for me, but often neither the tools to give me nor the strength to hold my trauma. So I learned to share only small pieces of my story selectively with friends as part of getting to know each other, but never in a way that put the weight of my story on them. I always knew the weight of my story, and having carried it all my life, I knew I could carry it, but I did not always know if they could. And not harming others is a core value for me.

Learning not to harm has been an important piece of learning to speak my story well. That withholding for the good of another has, at times, revealed my own strength and allowed me to care for friends and other survivors around the world like I want to.

Two notes on what I mean and don't mean when I talk about lessening possible harm connected to speaking my story.

One, the villains in our story, will always yell harm when we speak our stories out loud, but that is not the harm I am referencing. They created that possible end when they misused, abused, exploited, raped, and trafficked us. The truth becoming public may harm their cover story, but we are not responsible for damaging an image that was always an illusion.

The point I am making is not in relation to the villains in our lives but rather the friends and support systems we encounter. Our pain is never more important than the person in front of us. We don't want to inadvertently become the cause of harm. So, it is important to understand where friends fit in our lives and to honor them as the human gifts they are to us. They can love us, but they may not have the tools to help us heal and sometimes not even to hold the trauma of our stories, and that is ok.

Two, in relation to the survivor population, it is important to find the balance between giving trigger warnings and understanding that we cannot prevent all triggers. The world is a triggering place for trauma survivors, and we all have to learn how to handle our own triggers and how to move from triggered back to a place of centeredness and peace. We definitely can give people a heads-up that our story may be triggering, reinforce self-care tools, and always give people the option to leave or not listen. We just cannot cross that boundary into making ourselves responsible to keep those hearing and reading our stories away from all triggers and possible discomfort.

Support groups are another form of speaking with friends, and they are a good place to learn to share our stories with our peers who have the strength to hold our trauma. Support groups can have their problems, especially if our boundaries are low, but honestly, their strengths outweigh their weaknesses, though not all are created equal. The best support groups I have found are either those led by therapists or 12-step support groups.

The format of 12-step groups is what makes them so powerful. First, each person has an allotted time to share, which is important because, in a group setting, some people naturally overwhelm the group's time, but that is not allowed to happen in 12-step groups. Secondly, there is no cross-sharing, which means attempting to fix each other by speaking into the story just shared. This keeps everyone in their own story, working their own path, which is right where we need to be.

Support groups, friends, and therapists were where speaking my story out loud to safe people began. But for me, every moment of speaking has always been preceded and facilitated by writing my story.

While I adapted to processing out loud with people, I have always been primarily an internal processor, and writing is where I have spoken every piece of my story first. Writing is how I see and I have been writing my way out since I was 15.

When I was given that first journal when I was 15, I had no emotional vocabulary at all. So, I created my own emotional vocabulary of images and rhythm in poetry.

No one saw my poetry or writing for a few years, but it gave me something to point to, to say something about how this represents me and my reality right now. I couldn't have told you much more than that, but giving images of my feelings before I could even explain them in words was an important step in both my healing and paved a path to speak my story.

After I tried to kill myself when they assigned me to follow-up counseling, I spent a good 45 minutes a session with Violet in silence. Eventually, I learned that I could get over the wall inside me, blocking my words by writing her a note before my session so that we could discuss. Once I got something out there, then other words would follow. We used this pattern throughout my counseling with her until, with her help, I moved on to a safer land far away from where the land of my birth and trauma.

Writing was a workaround for me, a way around my walls, a way to boldly push past the fear of speaking my truth. It helped me to see first, and then it became a bridge to people around me. People had always been the source of my trauma, so understandably, there was a divide: walls and moats to cross to reach a connection with people.

Eventually, journaling, poetry and note writing gave way to another form of writing to help me speak my story and connect to the bigger issues it was connected to: blogging.

My first blog was set to private and was mostly a way to practice the idea of writing with the intent to share. This scared me at first, and I was way too metaphoric, using images in a poetic way that was too abstract for anyone to get the story behind it. My second blog continued on that theme and only had 12 followers, though I shared it regularly on social media.

Despite my overemphasis on metaphoric images and lack of specific details, it taught me how to write for people and to understand the internal impact of releasing my words into the world. Maybe it is because I had so much PTSD I was dealing with, but I found that I always experienced the impact of telling my story twice, once when I wrote it and once when I posted it. This blog eventually evolved, shifting the images to the side and allowing me to move into telling pieces of my story more articulately.

A few years later, as I faced and processed my trafficking trauma, I started blogging again. There were pieces of my story I wasn't ready to tell yet, but there were pieces I was ready to release into the world.

I began writing freelance. That was the start of speaking pieces of my story via blog to a much bigger audience. I learned to research and write about the issues underlying my story while also telling my story, and that combination is powerful. And it was during that season that I began the project that became the book that you have just finished.

When we are ready it is important to add our voice, our story into the world, into movements that bring change. Whether you write to speak like me or blurt it out and process it as you do, it's all part of the process of rising to speak our stories. If it is you speaking your story on your terms in your timing, keep at it.

Move from safe people and smaller circles outward, always adjusting as you feel your own strength to deal with any fallout. Never be pushed by any force to speak your story into the world before you are ready.

Writing my story of being trafficked in porn has been a 5-year writing project and simultaneously a five-year deep dive into healing. As I wrote each chapter, the ways I had been perceived and spun in porn were erased. The double exposure of broken perceptions that still haunted me deeply throughout years of healing came to an end as I finally saw my story and myself only through my own eyes.

Everyone has a different path to healing and speaking. Find yours.

www.ingramcontent.com/pod-product-compliance
Lightning Source LLC
Chambersburg PA
CBHW052142110526
44591CB00012B/1827